PRIMA'S OFFICIAL STRATEGY GUIDE

DEAN EVANS

Prima Games
A Division of Random House, Inc.

3000 Lava Ridge Court
Roseville, CA 95661
(916) 787-7000
www.primagames.com

The Prima Games logo is a registered trademark of Random House, Inc., registered in the United States and other countries. Primagames.com is a registered trademark of Random House, Inc., registered in the United States.

Project Editor: Jill Hinckley
Editorial Assistant: Etelvina Hernandez
Senior Product Manager: Sara E. Wilson

ISBN: 0-7615-3233-1
Library of Congress Catalog Card Number: 200100108064
Printed in the United States of America

01 02 03 04 BB 10 9 8 7 6 5 4 3 2 1

INTRODUCTION

"When they first said that they wanted me to break into a heavily fortified German base, past electrified fencing, trigger-happy sentries, and ravenous guard dogs, I didn't take them seriously. When they asked me again, I refused point-blank—I'd signed up to fight, not for a suicide run on my first combat mission. "Look," I said, "why can't the explosives guy do it?" They replied that they needed to get in quietly, without attracting attention. "What about the Spy?" I countered. But he was currently in a plane somewhere over the Atlantic and wouldn't get here until the morning. The top brass were insistent: They needed someone to get inside tonight.

"Which is why I now find myself clinging to a wall above two German sentries, hoping to God that I don't fall off. All I have to do is make it to the door of the building beneath me, negotiate any guards, and locate my contact, Natasha. Quietly does it. One wrong move and I'm history...."

Blending complex puzzles with squad-level tactical combat, *Commandos 2* presents you with an enormous gaming challenge. With 10 increasingly difficult missions to complete, there's very little room for error. If you lose even one of the soldiers under your command during a mission, you'll fail that mission and be forced to start again. Consequently, *Commandos 2* requires patience, strategic awareness, creativity, and timing. The importance of training and pre-planning is vital.

In the ancient teachings of celebrated Chinese strategist Sun Tzu, "It is foreknowledge that enables a brilliant ruler and an excellent leader to triumph over others wherever they move." In this guide, we've attempted to provide you with that crucial "foreknowledge." You'll learn about the Commandos that appear in the game, their skills, and how best to use them. Every weapon and item is examined in the "Stores" section, while strategies and tactics are revealed in the "Officer's Training" section. You'll be surprised what you can accomplish with just one Commando, a Knife, and a pack of Cigarettes.

After you've trained for the missions in *Commandos 2,* this guide provides detailed intelligence data on the landscapes and troops that you can expect to encounter. Once you know *how* to get the best out of your soldiers, you need to know *where* to go and *what* to do when you get there. Be aware of your surroundings and have the patience to reconnoitre, move, and act. The walkthroughs in this guide show you how to fully complete every mission and how to activate the 10 secret "bonus" missions that developer Pyro has hidden in the game. So what are you waiting for? Gather your troops and get going!

"Searchlights criss-crossed the surface of the water as the battle cruiser Leipzig *was nudged gently away from the dock by three smoke-belching tugs. She was one of the biggest ships in the German fleet, and had suffered only minor damage to her forward guns during her last engagement with the Royal Navy. The aging harbormaster smiled. With the* Leipzig *repaired and rearmed, the British ships would not stand a chance. Germany could win this war.*

As the harbormaster reached down for his coffee, he missed the explosion that ripped through the bow of the Leipzig, *below the waterline. A second blast rocked the battle cruiser moments later, then a third, sending towering plumes of fire and water into the sky. Before the final explosion, the great ship groaned and shuddered, listing slightly as screaming sailors hurled themselves into the water. Meanwhile, out beyond the harbour walls, a burly Commando helped his friend to clamber into their small, black rubber dinghy.*

"Enjoy the show?" asked the Diver taking of his goggles.

"Not bad, my friend," said his companion. "Not bad at all."

CONTENTS

CHAPTER 1

BASIC TRAINING

Commandos 2: Men of Courage retains the basic style and features of its predecessors, although there have been some tweaks and changes in gameplay. Each of the seven Commandos in the game—Green Beret, Thief, Sniper, Driver, Spy, Diver, Sapper—has his own unique weapons and skills. The Sapper, for example, is the only Commando who can use explosive weaponry, while the Thief can climb walls without using a ladder or a rope. In addition to the seven main commandos, there are two supporting characters to help you on your way—Natasha the Seductress, and Whiskey the dog.

Nevertheless, if you've played Commandos: Behind Enemy Lines or Commandos: Beyond the Call of Duty, you'll discover that some of the hotkeys have changed and that there are new characters and abilities to learn. One of the most important things you

need to do in *Commandos 2* is get the simple things right. Planning, quick thinking, and being handy with a Knife count for nothing if you can't bark clear and efficient orders to your troops.

THE INTERFACE

You control the game using a movement/ action cursor, while a sidebar on the right side of the display gives you one-click access to the game's major commands. This sidebar is fully activated when you right-click on one of the Commandos under your control. Looking from top to bottom, the sidebar consists of several buttons and indicators.

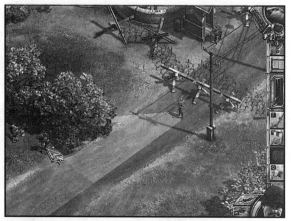

The sidebar on the right side of the screen gives you access to the selected Commando's commands.

FIELD OF VISION (Tab)

Clicking on the eye icon, or holding down Tab, changes the cursor into a Field of Vision icon. By left-clicking on any enemy soldier, you can view where he is currently looking. Enemies' range of vision is normally shown as a green cone. This changes to red when they have been alerted to your presence.

MAP (F9)

Next to the Field of Vision icon is the Map icon. Clicking this, or hitting F9, brings up a miniature overview of the mission landscape. Enemy soldiers are shown as red dots; allied soldiers and other Commandos are shown in blue. Mission objectives are shown as blue dots surrounded by a circle.

CAMERA (F12)

Located below the Field of Vision icon, the Camera allows you to fix the camera view onto a person, object, or location. Used with the multiple view options (F3 to F7), you can use this feature to watch an enemy soldier or keep an eye on your own Commandos while you examine another section of the game map.

HELP

Below the Camera is the Help icon. Clicking on this changes the cursor to a question mark. Clicking on an object, person, or item, links you directly to a description of it in the Notebook (if a description exists).

NOTEBOOK

The Notebook performs two main functions. Most importantly, clicking on it during a mission displays the list of Mission Goals. Click on an individual Mission Goal to bring up a graphic guide to its location. You can track the Mission Goal down with a combination of a Map view (with the helpful "The Objective Is Here" arrow), a zoomed-out view of the location, and a zoomed-in, detailed view of the location. Once you've clicked on a Mission Goal, you can close the Notebook and view an onscreen clue by

The built-in hint system shows the location of the captured soldier in THE GUNS OF YAKATONE mission.

clicking on the Clue icon that appears at the top of the screen. Doing so shows you the location of the previously selected Mission Goal and highlights it with an arrow. The second function of the Notebook is to provide descriptions of the main weapons and equipment, plus Commando abilities and other general game information. Click on the Contents tab to view this information.

STAMINA BAR

The Stamina Bar is an indication of how long a Commando can hang from a telephone wire or a wall, carry an object, swim underwater, etc. Thus, if the Stamina Bar runs out while a Commando is still hanging from a wall, he will fall, and if the Stamina Bar runs out while a Commando is still underwater, he will start to take damage and slowly drown.

BACKPACK

A Commando's Backpack shows which inventory items or actions are available for immediate use. For example, a Commando may start a mission equipped with a Pistol, but may want to use a Rifle when he eventually finds one. A Commando can only use items in his

inventory that have been equipped. To equip an item, either press the relevant hotkey (displayed next to its icon) or right-click on one of the four Backpack spaces to choose an alternative weapon or item. If a selected item can be activated remotely (for example, a Remote-Controlled Bomb or Decoy), an additional activation icon will also appear.

By right-clicking on a Backpack item, its alternatives will appear. Here, the Sapper can equip a Pistol rather than attack with his fists.

PORTRAIT

The Portrait does more than just show what your Commandos look like up close. Left-click on it to bring up icons of your available Commandos—these appear at the top of the screen and allow you to quickly switch among your troops with a single mouse-click. Also, by right-clicking on the Commando Portrait, you bring up that character's inventory. Icons on the inventory itself allow you to Swap items with other characters, Examine items in more detail, and Use items (such as a First Aid Kit).

HEALTH BAR

Next to the Portrait is the Health Bar. This is an indication of how much damage the selected soldier has taken. The Portrait also changes depending on how many hits a Commando has endured. A bloodied and bruised Green Beret, for example, needs healing with a First Aid Kit. Remember: You can't complete a mission if one of your Commandos dies.

ACTIONS

To the right of the Health Bar are icons representing the actions available to the selected Commando. Typically, the spaces here feature a Crawl/Stand icon and an Examine icon. Other actions that may appear here include: Dive, Standing Coverage, and Exit. We'll look at these in more detail over the next few pages.

MOVEMENT AND ACTIONS

Although you move your Commandos with the mouse, you can speed up control of them (and thus their reactions to danger) by mastering the hotkeys that activate the various actions. These hotkeys are listed in the Notebook.

Take control of more than one Commando by dragging a box around the ones you want to control.

MOVEMENT

To select a Commando, either right-click on his character on the main screen, click his Portrait, or press the relevant hotkey (for example, to control the Green Beret, press $\boxed{1}$). To move the selected Commando at a walking pace, left-click the location you wish the soldier to move to. To move the Commando at a run, double-click the intended location. The Commando automatically finds the quickest route to the selected point. By clicking on the Crawl icon at the bottom of the sidebar, or pressing $\boxed{\text{Spacebar}}$, you can drop your Commando into a prone position.

Finally, to multi-select Commandos and move them as a coordinated group, hold down the right mouse button and move the mouse to drag a box around them. All Commandos within the box will be selected. You also can select Commandos by holding down $\boxed{\text{Ctrl}}$ and clicking on their portraits at the top of

> **CAUTION**
> It's worth noting that the QUICKEST route may not be the SAFEST route. Running to a selected location also makes more noise than walking, which may attract the attention of any enemy guards.

the screen. Note that when you select multiple Commandos, they don't have access to their individual abilities—for example, the Green Beret can't stab an opponent if he's selected with another character. The characters can, however, crawl together, run, and shoot.

TIP

Hit the dirt! Staying low minimizes your chances of being seen by the enemy. Crawling may not get you anywhere fast, but it's often the best way to advance through enemy territory. Just remember, crawling limits your exposure to the enemy, but it also restricts what you can see and what you can attack.

GENERAL ACTIONS

Your Commandos can use items and interact with the game world in several different ways. The main options always appear in the Commando Actions section of the sidebar—for example, Crawl/Stand and Examine. To interact with objects or people in the game, use the [Shift] key. If you see an object lying on the ground, move the cursor over the item and hold down [Shift]. The cursor will change into a "grabbing hand" icon, and one more mouse click will pick the object up. Here are a few of the actions that can be performed with the [Shift] key:

ACTIONS USING [Shift]

ACTION	USED BY	DESCRIPTION
Pick up	All	Grab objects on the ground or pick up bodies
Examine	All	Search an item of furniture, box, crate, or body
Tie and Gag	All except Thief	Disable a stunned soldier
Open/Close Door	All	Provides entry and exit options to buildings, locations, and vehicles
Climb Wall	Thief only	The Thief can scale sheer walls when the Climb icon appears on the wall
Climb Telephone Pole	Thief, Green Beret	Commandos can use telephone wires to move above enemy guards without being seen
Climb Ladder	All	Provides access to new locations and rooms
Climb through Window	Thief, Green Beret	Provides these characters with another entry and exit option from buildings
Talk	All	Used to free captured characters and to complete Mission Goals
Use Wirecutters	Sapper only	Allows the Sapper to cut through wire fencing
Unlock Door/Crate	Thief only	Locked doors and boxes can be opened

ACTIONS USING [Shift] *CONTINUED*

ACTION	USED BY	DESCRIPTION
Activate Item	All	Used to throw switches, activate radios, etc.
Hide	Thief only	The Thief can hide in gaps between buildings, beneath beds, inside large chests, or under tables
Slip Through Hole	Thief only	Enables the Thief to crawl through small spaces

SPECIFIC ACTIONS

Commandos have a host of specific abilities or skills such as Stun, Steal from Enemy Soldier (Thief only), and Distract (Spy and Natasha only). Needless to say, if you click on an enemy soldier while holding a weapon, you get the opportunity to attack the enemy with the selected weapon. The movement cursor changes to a gun sight if you have a firearm equipped, a Knife icon if you want to attack with a Knife, or a fist should you wish to creep up behind a guard and knock him to the ground.

Rather than kill every enemy soldier, it's just as effective to knock them out and tie them up.

These specific abilities, along with the use of individual weapons and other vital Commando equipment, are addressed in Chapters 2 and 3.

CAMERA VIEW

The flexibility of the camera view in *Commandos 2* enables you to view the onscreen action from a range of angles and distances. For starters, by holding down [Alt] and pressing the left and right arrows, you can rotate the view in four directions: North, East, South, and West. You can also rotate the game view using the mouse—hold down [Alt] and left-click to rotate the view counterclockwise, right-click to rotate clockwise.

You can pan around the game world at any time by either using the cursor keys or by holding down [Alt] and moving the mouse. Using the [+] and [−] keys on the numeric keypad, you can zoom your chosen view in and out. Pressing [*] returns the view to its

optimal height. *Commandos 2* is playable in one of four different resolutions—640 × 480, 800 × 600, 1024 × 768, and 1280 × 1024 pixels. Additionally, there are four different levels of detail—Very Low, Low, Medium, and High. You can adjust the graphic complexity of the game to suit your computer by accessing the Video Options menu under the main Options menu.

Multiple camera views are also available in split screen modes (press F3 to F7), allowing you to watch several characters or areas of the mission map at once.

Use the Camera option on the sidebar to keep a target in view, then split the screen in two (F3) to keep an eye on your Commando AND the target.

SAVING THE GAME

Commandos 2 is difficult. Some missions may take you a few hours to complete, others an entire day. Maybe two days. Not only does the game have seven different Commandos, each with his own abilities and equipment, it also asks you to infiltrate bases and towns that are crammed full of enemy soldiers, snipers, tanks, and gun emplacements. We cannot stress enough the importance of regularly saving your game as you play through a mission. *Commandos 2* features a Quicksave option for this very purpose. Use it by pressing Ctrl - S .

CHAPTER 2

THE BARRACKS

Welcome to the Barracks. Here you can get an overview of the Commandos that you'll be using in the missions ahead. Each handpicked warrior has unique abilities and equipment. You will also learn a lot about the nature of a particular mission from the personnel assigned to you. For example, if a mission requires brute strength and brutal butchery, then the Green Beret is the perfect choice. Underwater work requires the Diver's talents, while setting or defusing explosives is what the Sapper is trained for. Joining them is the Driver (who can pilot or drive any vehicle), the Spy (who can disguise himself as the enemy), and the Sniper (the best sharpshooter the army has to offer).

New to *Commandos 2* is a seventh Commando, the Thief. This guy is a small and agile soldier trained in the arts of stealthy infiltration, picking locks, and picking pockets. Several supporting characters (including a dog) also have been incorporated into certain missions to help you out. Most missions in *Commandos 2* involve using the right character, at the right time, in the right place, with the right equipment. With this in mind, the better you know your Commandos, the better you know how to use them.

Only certain Commandos can use certain weapons. For example, only the Driver can throw Molotov Cocktails.

THE GREEN BERET ①

Highly skilled, the Green Beret is the best all-around grunt with the ability to use a wide range of weapons and objects. In most missions, he comes equipped with a Knife, Pistol, and a remote-controlled Decoy. He can quickly knock out and tie up guards, swing along telephone wires, and bury himself in soft ground to avoid detection. The Green Beret is the strongest of all the available Commandos, able to lift and move barrels and other heavy objects around the map. Use his talents as much as possible.

Name: Jerry McHale, a.k.a. "Tiny"

Date of birth: October 10, 1909

Place of birth: Dublin, Ireland

Current graduation: Sergeant

Height/Weight: 6'5"/220 lb

BACKGROUND

1929: Enlists in British Army

1934–37: Boxing champion in the British Army

1938: Condemned to 14 years forced labor in military prison for hitting a senior officer.

1940: His sentence is commuted when he joins the Commando Corps.

MILITARY RECORD

OPERATION ON THE ISLAND OF VAAGSO

Tiny is a silent killer, skilled at sneaking up behind enemies to stab them with the Knife.

Tiny was promoted to sergeant for his heroic actions. Cut off from his unit and without ammunition, he infiltrated a bunker and eliminated 16 enemy soldiers before returning to Allied lines.

INCURSION AT TMIMI AIRFIELD

Attacking one of the airfield's watchtowers with a bayonet while under enemy fire earned Tiny the Distinguished Service Medal. Despite receiving light wounds in one arm, he eliminated 15 enemy soldiers before being assisted by his comrades.

ADDITIONAL INFO

- Extremely violent character
- Serious disciplinary problems
- Great initiative and independence, combat behavior outstanding
- Expert at close combat and handling bladed weapons

NOTES

Tiny is the commando team leader. Because of his incredible ability to infiltrate enemy positions and silently neutralize threats to the team, you'll use him more than any other commando. The knife is his weapon of choice. His remote-control decoy is useful for distracting enemy soldiers' attention from himself or other commandos during a mission.

THE SNIPER ②

If you have the Sniper to command during a mission, you can bet that the enemy has one, too. Although the Sniper Rifle is completely silent and benefits from a long firing range, ammunition for it is severely limited. The Sniper might be able to carry as many as 25 rounds, but consider yourself fortunate if you start with more than three. Nevertheless, used wisely, the Sniper kills soldiers where other, quieter methods (stabbing and punching) fail. Keep the Sniper well out of harm's way until you really need it.

Name: Sir Francis T. Woolridge, a.k.a. "Duke"

Date of birth: March 21, 1909

Place of birth: Sheffield, England

Current graduation: Soldier

Height/Weight: 6'2"/180 lb

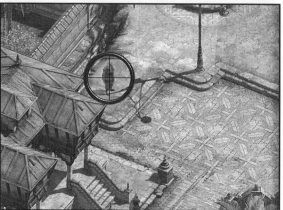

The Sniper is one of the most useful Commandos available to you. His skills, however, are balanced by limited ammunition.

BACKGROUND

Descended from a noble family, Woolridge is famous for his steady pulse.

1936: Earns gold medal in shooting at the Munich Olympics

1937: Enlists in British Army

1937–39: Stationed in India, recognized as an excellent marksman

1940: Joins the Commando Corps

MILITARY RECORD

AUCHINLECK OFFENSIVE

Woolridge is awarded a military medal for killing the commandant of the German garrison in Narvik, Norway with a single shot from a distance of more than a kilometer.

ADDITIONAL INFO

- Very reserved in his relationship with team members
- Cold and calculating character
- An expert marksman, extremely effective in situations of great tension

NOTES

While Duke's role in most missions is limited to eliminating enemy snipers and distant enemies with his sniper rifle, he can also be used to provide covering fire or to ambush using all types of firearms. His sniper rifle has limited ammunition, but he can pick up enemy sniper rifles and ammo from dead snipers. He usually stays back while the rest of the team advances, then moves forward when his one-shot-one-kill ability is needed

THE DIVER 3

The Diver is much more than just an underwater specialist. Like the Green Beret, he's a good, all-around Commando who's usually equipped with a Knife, Diving Gear, Harpoon Gun, and a Grappling Hook. The Diver's great strength is his skill with the blade. Unlike the Green Beret, the Diver uses his Knife as a throwing weapon, enabling him to silently take down enemy soldiers from a short distance. Give him more than one Knife and he becomes a lethal killer. You might even find yourself using him more than the Green Beret.

Name: James Blackwood, a.k.a. "Fins"

Date of birth: August 3, 1911

Place of birth: Melbourne, Australia

Current graduation: Soldier

Height/Weight: 6'1"/181 lb

Skills: Invaluable in naval operations

BACKGROUND

This naval engineer studied at Oxford. For three consecutive years he was a member of the rowing team that won the Henley Regatta competition between Oxford and Cambridge universities. A great swimmer, he was the first person to swim the English Channel (on a bet).

Use the Diver for more than just underwater tasks; his skills with a Knife are excellent.

1935: Enlists in Royal Navy

1936: Promoted to captain

1938: Degraded to sergeant due to an "incident" during a stopover in Hawaii

1940: Given option of joining Commando Corps as an ordinary soldier or being expelled from the Armed Forces after further conduct problems

MILITARY RECORD

DUNKIRK

Blackwood is awarded the Military Cross for his heroic behavior in rescuing 45 soldiers surrounded on a beach and facing capture.

ADDITIONAL INFO

- A dissolute character who loves a good time
- Great gambler
- Alcohol problems "apparently" under control
- Invaluable nautical skills in any mission that involves naval operations

NOTES

Although all the commandos can swim, Fins' use of an underwater breathing device allows him to stay submerged and swim right under the enemy's nose without being detected. His spear gun is the only silent ranged weapon in the commando arsenal and allows him to stealthily eliminate enemies near the water as well as on land. Fins is the only commando who can operate marine craft.

THE SAPPER ④

Not only can the Sapper handle Timed Bombs, Remote-Controlled Bombs, Grenades, Mines, and Anti-Tank Mines, he's also trained to use a Flame Thrower, Blowtorch, and Bazooka. If you find any heavy weaponry, only the Sapper can use it. He also carries a Mine Detector to locate and defuse explosives placed by the enemy, and a set of Wirecutters to snip through barbed wire and mesh fencing. If you don't have access to a Sapper in a particular mission, don't bother picking up any explosives.

Name: Thomas Hancock, a.k.a. "Inferno"

Date of birth: January 14, 1911

Place of birth: Liverpool, England

Current graduation: Soldier

Height/Weight: 6'/175 lb

BACKGROUND

1933: Joined the fire department in his hometown (Liverpool)

1934: Joined the high-risk Explosives Department

1939: Joined the British Army

1940: Volunteered for the Commando Corps

The Sapper is the only one of the seven Commandos who uses explosives—including Grenades.

MILITARY RECORD

OPERATION CHARIOT

During the assault on St. Nazaire, Fins orchestrated the explosions that caused many casualties in the German garrison and rendered the port installation useless for many months. Captured during the operation, he managed to escape (after four attempts in just two months) and return to England.

ADDITIONAL INFO

- Outstanding valor and daring, sometimes rash behavior
- Extensive knowledge and experience with explosives
- Specializes in creation of explosives using almost any material

NOTES

Inferno's expertise with all types of explosives is vital for several types of missions. In addition to placing bombs, he can also use grenades and the PIAT bazooka. Both are great for taking out enemy troop concentrations. Inferno can employ a mine detector to locate and disarm mines, then can use them against the enemy.

THE DRIVER ⑤

Driver by name, driver by nature. But the talents of this much undervalued Commando doesn't stop at the vehicular. Not only can he handle tanks and planes, but he can also use Molotov Cocktails, Gas and Smoke Grenades, the Trap and the Trip Wire. The Driver can also handle a Shovel and dig small holes in a matter of minutes. If you don't have a Sapper in your Commando squad, the Driver makes a half-decent replacement.

Name: Sid Perkins, a.k.a. "Tread"
Date of birth: April 4, 1910
Place of birth: Brooklyn, USA
Current graduation: Soldier
Height/Weight: 6'2"/183 lb

BACKGROUND

Long criminal career involving car theft, armed robbery, and similar crimes in the USA.

1937: Flees to England to avoid a prison term

1938: Evades pursuing American authorities by enlisting in the British Army

1938–40: Collaborates with the Foreign Office to test vehicles and arms captured from the enemy

1941: Meets Paddy Maine, who recruits him for the Commando Corps

The Driver might seem like the least useful of all the Commandos, but he has hidden talents.

MILITARY RECORD

TAMET AIRFIELD

In assaulting the Tamet Airfield with the LRDG, Perkins destroyed eight German fighter planes with his jeep's machine guns, and with no ammunition left, eliminated four more by smashing his vehicle into them. Suffered severe burns.

ADDITIONAL INFO

- Somewhat untrustworthy in the eyes of the other commandos; he does not have a good relationship with his teammates.
- Extensive mechanical knowledge, able to drive and repair all types of land vehicles
- Considerable skill at handling all types of arms, acquired during his Foreign Office duty

NOTES

Tread is often used as the getaway driver for the commandos' missions. However, his ability to hot-wire a tank can give the team some heavy firepower they'd normally lack. Skilled with all types of firearms, Tread can also be used for covering fire and ambushes to support other team members.

THE SPY 6

The Spy can use a Pistol, Rifle, or Machine-gun, but he's best used to distract enemy soldiers. Unlike the other Commandos, he can wear German and Japanese uniforms for long periods of time, and can successfully talk to lower-ranking soldiers. Dressed as an officer, the Spy can even issue orders to soldiers and Lieutenants to make them look or move in a different direction. The Spy carries a Hypodermic Syringe filled with poison that he can use to daze, drug, or kill enemy guards.

Name: Rene Duchamp, a.k.a. "Spooky"

Date of birth: November 20, 1911

Place of birth: Lyon, France

Current graduation: Soldier

Height/Weight: 6'4"/179 lb

BACKGROUND

1934: Joins French secret service

1935–38: Chief of security at the French embassy, Berlin

1939: Enlists in the French army at the start of the war

1940: Joins the French resistance after German invasion, contacted by the Commando Corps, collaborates occasionally with British commandos in special operations

The Spy is one of the most useful Commandos. He makes getting into the most well-guarded bases a little bit easier.

MILITARY RECORD

Duchamp has participated in numerous sabotage operations and is responsible for destroying at least three trains, fourteen tanks, and over thirty land vehicles. His information about German troop positions and movement is invaluable to the British secret service.

ADDITIONAL INFO

- Amiable character, great at conversation
- Feels absolute hatred for the Nazis
- Expertise in communications and techniques of infiltration and sabotage acquired in secret service
- Speaks French, German, English, Russian, and Italian fluently

NOTES

Spooky is the only commando who can put on an enemy uniform, walk up to enemy soldiers, and engage them in conversation. His disguise ability allows him to infiltrate enemy installations and/or distract soldiers so that teammates can complete their objectives. Using a syringe filled with poison, Spooky can kill silently.

NATASHA ⑦

Like the Spy, Natasha can be used to wander freely around enemy territory— as long as she doesn't do anything suspicious. "Armed" with different outfits and Lipstick, her main benefit to you, the Commander of the Commandos, is to distract enemy soldiers. Her attacking options are much more limited than the Spy (although her main advantage is that she can handle a Sniper Rifle). She's best used to scout the interiors of buildings, allowing you to gain vital intelligence about enemy numbers before you mount an attack with your Commandos.

Name: Natasha Nikochevski, a.k.a. "Lips"
Date of birth: April 21, 1912
Place of birth: Kiev, Ukraine
Current graduation: Lieutenant
Height/Weight: 5'8"/130 lb

BACKGROUND

1928: Enters the Soviet intelligence service

1934: Achieves rank of sharpshooter in the Red Army

1935: Sent to Siberia after a murky incident with a political commissar

1940: Goes to Germany with orders to obtain information regarding a possible German attack on the USSR

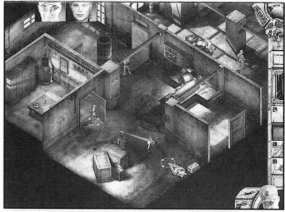

Natasha is a Dutch resistance contact who performs a "disguise and distract" role that's similar to the Spy's.

MILITARY RECORD

OPERATION BARBAROSSA

Thanks to her investigations in Berlin, a surprise attack on Minsk is disrupted.

OPERATION ZHUKOV

She assassinated General von Graufftend after avoiding his entire personal guard and is decorated with the Order of Lenin.

SIEGE OF LENINGRAD

Sniping while camouflaged among the ruins of the city, she manages to destroy two enemy battalions and thus permits the evacuation of a field hospital. For this she receives the Legion of Honor from the Committee.

ADDITIONAL INFO

- Young lady of aristocratic background, educated in the best schools
- Cold and calculating
- Knowledge of various European languages and social habits, able to establish relationships with enemy easily
- Impetuous and overpowering, subjected to various disciplinary measures by displeased superiors

NOTES

Natasha operates similarly to Spooky; she is able to walk right past enemies and even distract their attention away from the actions of the rest of the team.

THE THIEF ⑧

Small, fast-moving, and agile, the Thief is the last member of the Commando team. Typically equipped with a Lockpick, the Thief has the ability to climb sheer walls and pick locks. Additionally, the Thief can also use the Wirecutters and carry a portable Ladder (allowing others to follow him over small walls). Note that while the Thief can knock out enemy soldiers, he doesn't have the ability to tie them up. He can, however, steal items from opponents without being spotted, jump through windows, and crawl through small spaces. He also has a distracting pet rat named Spike.

Not only can the Thief stick to walls, he's also skilled at picking locked doors and unlocking boxes.

Name: Paul Toledo, a.k.a. "Lupin"

Date of birth: March 1, 1916

Place of birth: Paris, France

Current graduation: Soldier

Height/Weight: 5'2"/107 lb

BACKGROUND

1916–28: Raised in a suburban Parisian orphanage, runs away at age 10 and joins the infant pickpocket gang, arrested at age 12 and locked away in the remand home

1928–34: Engaged in multiple, far-reaching robberies while involved in spectacular flights from reformatories

1935–39: Known by the nickname "Lupin," becomes a Parisian underworld legend of thievery, charged with big thefts from museums, jewelers, and art galleries despite lack of evidence

1940: Betrayed by an accomplice, caught selling loot to a Dutch receiver, sentenced to 15 years in a maximum security prison

1940: Escapes prison when bombarded by the German army during the invasion

1940–41: Joins French resistance, specializes in removal of important artwork from grasp of Nazis

1941 April: Recruited by the Gestapo, assaults the Louvre and steals 37 paintings, flees to England, attempts to join DeGaulle's Free French Forces and is rejected because of criminal past

1941 May: Meets Paddy Maine, who recruits him to the Commandos Corps

ADDITIONAL INFO

- Exceptional speed and agility
- Not fond of guns, uses them only if forced
- Reserved but loyal, quickly gains friendship from fellow commandos

NOTES

Very quick, Lupin can be used to run right past the enemy. His ability to stand right behind a soldier while staying out of sight allows him to pick the enemy's pockets for useful items. Lupin is the only commando who can pick locks, allowing him to open doors or steel cases containing weapons and other equipment.

WHISKEY ⑨

Whiskey appears in several missions throughout *Commandos 2,* along with the silent Whistles that characters use to summon him. Whiskey can distract guards by barking—although the effect is only temporary. He's best used to ferry items between Commandos that have been separated on a mission map—for example, Das Boot. Whiskey can also sniff out mines. Unfortunately, he hasn't yet learned how to defuse them.

Name: Whiskey

Date of birth: Approximately 1935

Place of birth: Unknown

Current graduation: Indeterminate
Height/Weight: 18"/65 lb

BACKGROUND

1941: Picked up by the Commandos during a mission after his owner died

1941: Enlisted as a mascot for the Commando Corps

ADDITIONAL INFO

- Exceptionally loyal, is considered the same as any other commando
- Strong and fast
- Extremely fierce when the situation warrants

Man's best friend is less a doggie Commando and more a personalized, four-legged courier service.

NOTES

Whiskey can walk right past enemy soldiers without causing alarm. The team can use this ability to send weapons and equipment from one team member to another, right past an unwitting enemy. Each commando is issued a dog whistle for calling Whiskey to his or her position.

WILSON ⑨

Wilson, a shipwrecked sailor, can be found stranded on the island you need to infiltrate in the Guns of Yakatone mission. Like Whiskey, Wilson can be used to divert enemy soldiers temporarily and to store those extra items that your Commandos can't carry. Like Natasha, Wilson can be given a gun to help out in combat when needed. Remember—if a mission features an extra character such as this, he or she is there for a reason.

Wilson is one of several supporting characters who you can use to distract the enemy and help your Commandos.

CHAPTER 3
THE STORES

Your Commandos can use a wide range of equipment, from familiar weaponry like Machineguns and Rifles to more obscure items such as Traps, Molotov Cocktails, and highly trained, dancing rodents. What makes *Commandos 2* challenging to play, however, is that not every Commando can use every weapon or item in the game. Each of the seven Commandos has his own unique skills and equipment—the Green Beret and the Diver can wield the Knife, for example, but the Sapper is the only Commando trained to use high explosives.

In this chapter, we examine what you can do with the items featured in the game and tell you who can use them effectively. There's no point in carrying around a Bazooka that you've stolen if you don't have the Sapper in your team to fire it. It takes up four valuable spaces in one of your Commando's inventories. More than 40 weapons and items are available to your troops as they stab, shoot, and fast-talk their way through the various missions. The key to success is knowing which items to take with you and which to leave behind.

Pay attention, soldier! This information will save your life.

WEAPONS

PISTOL

Several of your Commandos will be equipped with the Colt 1911A Pistol as a standard. Despite its unlimited ammunition, don't rely on it for regular combat—you can use Rifles and Machineguns that you pick up from enemy soldiers. Typically, you need to fire three shots with a Pistol to take out an opponent. German and Japanese versions (with limited ammo) are also available.

Used by: All

Inventory size: 1 space

Maximum charges/shots: Unlimited

RIFLE

Allied soldiers use the Lee Enfield Rifle, but Commandos can scavenge the similar Karabiner 98K from the bodies of enemy soldiers. Hampered by a slow reload time, the Karabiner has the firepower to kill with one shot. It does, however have limited ammunition. Do not use it in missions in which stealth is paramount.

Used by: All

Inventory size: 4 spaces

Maximum charges/shots: 15

SNIPER RIFLE

The M1903.30 Springfield Sniper Rifle and its German
equivalent, the Gewehr 98, are two of the most effective guns in *Commandos 2*.
To balance out their long-range capabilities and one-shot stopping power, ammunition
for these weapons is scarce. Use a Sniper's bullets wisely until you can pick up more
from dead enemy sharpshooters.

Used by: Sniper, Natasha

Inventory size: 4 spaces

Maximum charges/shots: 25

MACHINEGUN

The MP40 Machinegun comes in handy if you want to take down
several charging enemies at once. Capable of firing wide-angle bursts of
gunfire, the Machinegun is never issued as standard and must always
be stolen from the enemy. Despite its limited ammunition, it is very
effective when used with the Standing Coverage command (see Chapter 4).

Used by: All

Inventory size: 4 spaces

Maximum charges/shots: 150

KNIFE

Because most of the missions in *Commandos 2* require a stealthy
approach, the Fairburn Combat Knife will be your primary weapon. Only
two of your Commandos can wield it, though—the Green Beret uses it as
a stabbing weapon, while the Diver throws it at his enemies. Although the
Green Beret needs only one Knife, the Diver can carry and use several of them.

Used by: Green Beret, Diver

Inventory size: 1 space

Maximum charges/shots: —

BAZOOKA

The PIAT Bazooka, or rocket launcher, is a formidable heavy weapon. It is available when your Commandos are likely to encounter vehicle-based threats such as tanks and armored cars. Only the Sapper can use the Bazooka in the field. The weapon swallows four inventory spaces, as does the ammunition it requires.

Used by: Sapper

Inventory size: 8 spaces

Maximum charges/shots: 6

HAND GRENADE

Hardly the stealthiest of weapons, the Grenade is a vital weapon for quickly taking out groups of enemy soldiers. Used by the Sapper, throw these No.36M MK1 "Mills Bombs" through doorways and windows to quickly clear rooms and bunkers. Only use a Grenade in the open when you're sure that half the opposing army won't come running to investigate.

Used by: Sapper

Inventory size: 1 space

Maximum charges/shots: 10

SMOKE GRENADE

Although it lacks any real destructive power, the Smoke Grenade is very effective in providing cover for advancing Commandos. Used only by the Driver, this non-lethal weapon creates a cloud of thick smoke that your soldiers can use to mask themselves from the enemy. This is useful if you need to cross an open space without being spotted.

Used by: Driver

Inventory size: 1 space

Maximum charges/shots: 10

GAS GRENADE

Like the Smoke Grenade, the Gas Grenade doesn't kill or injure enemy troops. Think of it as a wide-angle "punch" that, once thrown, knocks out soldiers in the targeted area. Fortunately, Allied soldiers are not affected. The Gas Grenade offers a quieter solution than the Grenade to the room clearance problem. Its availability, however, is limited.

Used by: Driver

Inventory size: 1 space

Maximum charges/shots: 10

MOLOTOV COCKTAIL

These gasoline-based fire bombs also make good alternatives to Grenades— especially if your mission team lacks a Sapper. The multi-talented Driver can throw the Molotov through windows and doorways just like a Grenade. Its area of effect is slightly smaller, but it's no less effective.

Used by: Driver

Inventory size: 1 space

Maximum charges/shots: 10

REMOTE-CONTROLLED BOMB

This "smart" explosive consists of two parts—the bomb and a remote detonator. Used only by the Sapper, it's a good alternative to the Timed Bomb because it gives your Commando team more control over *when* the bomb explodes. Once set, a detonator icon appears next to the Backpack spaces on the Sapper's sidebar. Click it to set off the charge.

Used by: Sapper

Inventory size: 4 spaces

Maximum charges/shots: 1

TIMED BOMB

This explosive charge is your basic "set it, then run like hell" device. There's very little finesse involved when using a Timed Bomb. After it's placed, the Commandos have 20 seconds to get away before it explodes. When a bomb is detonated, enemy soldiers will run to investigate. So, you can also use these bombs as diversions.

Used by: Sapper

Inventory size: 2 spaces

Maximum charges/shots: 1

MINES

Not only can the Sapper locate and defuse hidden enemy landmines, he also can pick them up and reuse them. Once placed by a Sapper, the Mines are visible (and inactive) to Allied soldiers, but invisible (and active) to the enemy. Any soldier who gets too close to a landmine automatically sets it off. Use Mines to block off key enemy attack or rally points.

Used by: Sapper

Inventory size: 1 space

Maximum charges/shots: 10

ANTI-TANK MINES

A bigger version of the basic Mine, the Anti-Tank Mine is triggered only when a vehicle such as a tank or armored car drives over it. Like the anti-personnel Mine, these explosives can be detected, defused, then reused by the Sapper. Anti-Tank Mines are particularly useful in the Saving Private Smith mission.

Used by: Sapper

Inventory size: 1 space

Maximum charges/shots: 10

HYPODERMIC SYRINGE

Issued as a standard to the Spy, the Hypodermic Syringe is a silent weapon that allows the master infiltrator to contribute to the mission's body count. Refilled with bottles of Poison that can be found across the mission maps, the Syringe has different effects on victims depending on the dosage administered. One jab temporarily dazes soldiers, a second knocks them out, a third is lethal.

Used by: Spy

Inventory size: 1 space

Maximum charges/shots: 15

FLAME THROWER

Although it's not widely available, the Flame Thrower is a devastating weapon combining the accuracy of a firearm with the fiery joys of a Molotov Cocktail. Only the Sapper can use this heavy weapon, so don't carry it in missions in which you don't have access to him. The Flame Thrower also works best when fired on *level* ground.

Used by: Sapper

Inventory size: 4 spaces

Maximum charges/shots: 500

HARPOON GUN

The Harpoon Gun is issued to the Diver when underwater work forms a significant part of the mission. Think of it as an aquatic Pistol, with the same short-firing range and unlimited ammunition. Useful against enemy divers, crocodiles, and sharks, the Harpoon Gun does *not* function on dry land. So, if you don't need it, drop it to make room for more useful items.

Used by: Diver

Inventory size: 2 spaces

Maximum charges/shots: Unlimited

EQUIPMENT

BARRELS

Although you can't add these large metal drums to a Commando's inventory, you can lift and move them around a mission map. The Barrels in *Commandos 2* are highly explosive and you can detonate them by shooting at them or blowing up a bomb nearby. Mines and Barrels make a fun and deadly combo....

Used by: Green Beret

Inventory size: —

Maximum charges/shots: 1

BINOCULARS

By activating the Leica SLC 8×56 Binoculars and clicking on a soldier, you can view his rank, the type of weapon he carries, whether he leaves his position, and how much health he has left. Such information can be vital when planning an attack.

Used by: All

Inventory size: 1 space

Maximum charges/shots: —

BLOWTORCH

The Blowtorch is another specialized item. When it's included in a mission, it's there for a reason. You can use the Blowtorch to fix broken objects and cut open metal doors. In the Saving Private Smith mission, for example, you use it to get inside the plane that has crashed in the river.

Used by: Sapper, Driver

Inventory size: 2 spaces

Maximum charges/shots: —

CIGARETTES

Along with the Knife, packets of Cigarettes are one of the most important items that a Commando can carry. In fact, with these two items alone, you can often lure and stab your way through whole garrisons of soldiers. For more information about the enemy's love of a good smoke, see Chapter 4.

Used by: All

Inventory size: 1 space

Maximum charges/shots: 10

DECOY

Although the Decoy is typically issued to the Green Beret, any Commando can use it. The machine consists of two parts—the Philips L12 emitter and the remote control that activates it. Like Cigarettes and Wine Bottles, the Decoy is used to lure enemy soldiers away from their positions.

Used by: All

Inventory size: 3 spaces

Maximum charges/shots: —

DIVING GEAR

The Diver's all-important Diving Gear is issued whenever a mission features water for this Commando to swim in. Clicking on the Diving Gear orders the Diver to change into his wetsuit and SCUBA gear, equipment that allows him to stay underwater for long periods.

Used by: Diver

Inventory size: 2 spaces

Maximum charges/shots: —

DOG FOOD

You can feed these large chunks of raw meat to the guard dogs that patrol some of the more heavily protected German compounds. Guard dogs act in much the same way as their human counterparts, although in addition to being alerted by the sight and sound of you, they can also smell you coming.

Used by: All

Inventory size: 1 space

Maximum charges/shots: 1

NOTE

By using Sleeping Pills, a Commando can poison Dog Food (turning it from red to green). The resulting Poisoned Dog Food is used to distract, divert, and ultimately disable a guard dog. The dogs will then stay asleep for the duration of the mission.

FIRST AID KIT

If you plan to pursue a more open, trigger-happy strategy in *Commandos 2,* your troops will get injured. First Aid Kits are scattered across the mission maps. Each one provides a boost to a Commando's Health Bar. The amount they restore depends on the difficulty level you choose.

Used by: All

Inventory size: 2 spaces

Maximum charges/shots: Varies

FISH FOOD

By using Fish Food underwater, the Diver and Green Beret can create an organic Smoke Grenade. Activating the Fish Food attracts nearby shoals of fish that swim around the submerged Commando, obscuring him from nearby enemies. Unlike smoke, however, the fish shoal moves *with* the Commando.

Used by: All

Inventory size: 1 space

Maximum charges/shots: 1

GRAPPLING HOOK

You mainly use the Grappling Hook to help the Diver scale low walls, but you can also use it as a Trip Wire. The Grappling Hook is vital if your Commando unit has no access to the climbing skills that the Thief possesses. It proves that there's more to the Diver than his underwater talents.

Used by: Diver

Inventory size: 4 spaces

Maximum charges/shots: —

LADDER

The Ladder is typically carried by the Thief who, after he has climbed a sheer wall, can lower it for the other Commandos to use. Use the Ladder outside and inside buildings (that is, drop it out of a window). You can only pick up the Ladder again from above.

Used by: All

Inventory size: 4 spaces

Maximum charges/shots: —

LIPSTICK

The Lipstick is part of Natasha's basic inventory. Using it allows her to distract enemy soldiers, just as the Spy uses his Distract skill. Once activated, the movement cursor becomes a Lipstick icon. When this icon is clicked on an enemy soldier, the victim turns to face Natasha and stays there until the command is canceled by right-clicking on your mouse.

Used by: Natasha

Inventory size: 1 space

Maximum charges/shots: —

LOCKPICK

Issued standard to the Thief, the Lockpick enables the agile wall-crawler to open locked doors and metal ammunition crates. Once opened by the Thief, any other Commando can use previously locked doors. Doors typically are locked from the inside, so the Thief must enter buildings via other routes (such as a window) to unlock them.

Used by: Thief

Inventory size: 1 space

Maximum charges/shots: —

MINE DETECTOR

The Mine Detector is standard issue for the Sapper in most missions and, unless Whiskey the dog is part of the team, it's the only way of detecting Mines and Anti-Tank Mines. After you locate these buried explosives, the Sapper can defuse them and pick them up for later use.

Used by: Sapper

Inventory size: 3 spaces

Maximum charges/shots: —

NATASHA'S CLOTHING

Like the Spy, Natasha can wear disguises that allow her to move freely (and undetected) through enemy territory. In the Das Boot mission, for example, she is dressed as a German secretary, allowing her to enter all buildings, to operate switches, search furniture, and distract enemy soldiers.

Used by: Natasha

Inventory size: 4 spaces

Maximum charges/shots: —

POISON BOTTLE

The Poison Bottle adds two doses of Poison to the Spy's Hypodermic Syringe. Typically, the Spy starts a mission with as little as three doses in his unique weapon. This "ammunition" must be picked up during a mission and is found in furniture and wooden boxes scattered across the mission map.

Used by: Spy

Inventory size: 1 space

Maximum charges/shots: 2

SHEET LADDER

You use this Ladder variant in the Colditz mission, where Commandos must use limited equipment to complete their mission objectives. By linking the Sheets together, the Commandos can construct a rudimentary rope that performs a function similar to the standard-issue Ladder.

Used by: All

Inventory size: 4 spaces

Maximum charges/shots: —

SHOVEL

Not to be confused with the Green Beret's Bury ability, the Shovel is issued to the Driver. With this item in his inventory, the Driver can quickly dig deep holes to trap and dispose of enemy soldiers. See Chapter 4 for more details about this fun tactic.

Used by: Driver

Inventory size: 2 spaces

Maximum charges/shots: —

SLEEPING PILLS

You use bottles of Sleeping Pills with two other items in the game. First, use them to poison Wine Bottles as a way of distracting and knocking out enemy soldiers. Second, combine them with Dog Food to send guard dogs safely to sleep.

Used by: All

Inventory size: 1 space

Maximum charges/shots: Varies

SNOW GEAR

Snow Gear consists of a thermal suit that your Commandos must wear when they operate in subzero conditions. Specifically, you need Snow Gear for the Ice mission or your Commandos will die when they go outside. Commandos can wear enemy snow uniforms. But, like normal enemy uniforms, these only last for a limited time.

Used by: All

Inventory size: 0

Maximum charges/shots: —

SPIKE

Spike is a pet rat, highly trained by the Thief to perform simple but effective tricks. Like Whiskey the dog, Spike can be used to distract an enemy soldier temporarily, allowing the Thief or another Commando to slip by unnoticed. Once used, Spike returns to the Thief.

Used by: Thief

Inventory size: —

Maximum charges/shots: —

CANNED FOOD

Think of Canned Food as a mini–First Aid Kit. Scattered generously across the mission maps, these items regenerate your Commandos' lowered health levels. Unlike the First Aid Kit, however, the boost that Canned Food gives an injured Commando is small.

Used by: All

Inventory size: 1 space

Maximum charges/shots: 1

TRAP

Although the Trap is a large, rusting set of metal jaws, after you place it on the ground it becomes invisible to the enemy. It kills any soldier who steps on it, but needs to be picked and reset before it can be used again. Only the Driver can use this offbeat weapon.

Used by: Driver

Inventory size: 2 spaces

Maximum charges/shots: —

TRIP WIRE

Issued to the Driver, the Trip Wire is one of the more specialized devices that *Commandos 2* offers your troops. Stretch it across a doorway or path—any enemy soldier who walks into it falls and is rendered unconscious. Using the Trip Wire is a good way to incapacitate individual soldiers if you're attacked by a group of enemies. Note that the Trip Wire will *not* affect alerted soldiers.

Used by: Driver

Inventory size: 1 space

Maximum charges/shots: 1

UNIFORMS

Although all Commandos can wear enemy uniforms, only the Spy can wear them for long periods of time. There are three different types or ranks in the game—soldier, Lieutenant, and Officer. Only the Spy can wear Lieutenant and Officer uniforms.

Used by: All

Inventory size: 4 spaces

Maximum charges/shots: 100

WINE BOTTLE

Like packets of Cigarettes, Wine Bottles can distract enemy soldiers and draw them out of position (see Chapter 4). It's always worthwhile to carry one Wine Bottle. Officers are more susceptible to this free alcohol than lower-ranking Lieutenants and soldiers.

Used by: All

Inventory size: 1 space

Maximum charges/shots: 1

NOTE
Using the Sleeping Pills, a Commando can poison a Wine Bottle (turning it from red to green). You can use the resulting Poisoned Wine Bottle to distract, divert, and ultimately disable an enemy soldier. After they're unconscious, tie and gag them.

WIRECUTTERS

Although this item typically is issued to the Sapper, all of the Commandos can use the Wirecutters to snip through barbed wire fences and mesh fencing. It's always useful to have a pair of Wirecutters in a mission. They are found in stores, garages, or on the bodies of mechanics.

Used by: All

Inventory size: 2 spaces

Maximum charges/shots: —

WHISTLE

Whenever Whiskey is included in a mission, each Commando in your team is issued a silent dog Whistle for summoning him. Use the Whistles and Whiskey to ferry items and supplies among your Commandos.

Used by: All

Inventory size: 1 space

Maximum charges/shots: —

CHAPTER 4

OFFICER TRAINING

At ease, soldier. In the last three chapters, you've met your Commandos and familiarized yourself with the weapons and items that you'll encounter in the field. In this, the final phase of your training, we'll be dealing with the art of war—how to plan attacks, how to execute attacks, and how to react to the consequences of your actions.

In *Commandos 2,* planning a mission isn't quite as simple as noting the objectives and finding the best way to reach them. If your objective is to free a submarine crew, as it is in the Das Boot mission, you need to do more than just make it to the building where the crew is being held. You also have to find the guard who holds the key. Principle objectives in *Commandos 2* often require several sub-objectives to be completed beforehand. These objectives may take the combined efforts of several characters or acts of heroism by a lone Commando. Although you can plan how you'd *like* the mission to go, it will never be perfect. Ultimately, you've got to be flexible enough to react to the changing situation as the mission unfolds.

This chapter offers a look at the key elements of successful mission planning and execution. Keep in mind though: What you need most when playing *Commandos 2* is *patience*.

RECONNAISSANCE

Preparation is the key to success in *Commandos 2*. You don't just need to know your own troops' capabilities. It's also important to know the enemy's strengths and weaknesses. In many respects, each mission is like a puzzle. As the commander, your job is to make sure that all the pieces are in the right place.

WHICH COMMANDOS?

In each of the missions, you're assigned some or all of the Commandos shown in Chapter 2. You get certain Commandos for a reason—for example, you might get a Spy because you can't complete the mission without being able to walk undetected among enemy soldiers, or you might need a Sapper to handle high explosives. You can tell a lot about a mission by the personnel that you're given to complete it. The Das Boot at Night mission, for example, initially gives you only the Thief to control.

The Commandos you're assigned for a mission give you an indication of what to expect.

This indicates that you should complete the first objective using a lot of sneaking around and very little actual combat. The Paris mission, in contrast, gives you all seven Commandos—so you know you're in for a struggle.

TAKE A LOOK AROUND

Before moving your Commandos, take some time to study the landscape. Use ⊞ and ⊟ to zoom the 3D view out as far as it will go and pan the immediate area using the cursor keys. Note the locations of nearby enemy soldiers—rotate the view to get a better understanding of where the threats are in relation to your start point. Hold down [F11] to highlight the soldiers, Lieutenants, Officers, guard dogs, and other threats on the landscape. This method lets you see every exterior enemy, even those behind buildings, trees, or walls. It doesn't, however, let you spy inside buildings.

THE MISSION MAP

Use [F9] to bring up the Mission Map. This satellite-style angle gives you a zoomed-out overhead view, overlaid with the positions of enemy and Allied soldiers—red dots are enemy soldiers, while friendly units are shown in blue. With this information, you can instantly see where the target area has the fewest defenses, where the troops are concentrated, and what you might need to do to counter them.

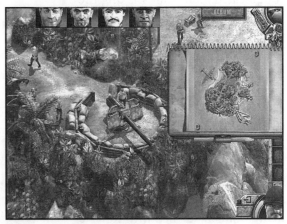

Use the Mission Map ([F9]) to see where the enemies are strongest.

MISSION OBJECTIVES

Once you've scanned the landscape and noted the positions of the enemy, familiarize yourself with the objectives. *Commandos 2* has a new feature that allows you to view several graphical guides to enemy locations, including a Map view, zoomed-out view, and zoomed-in view. The questions you then need to ask are: Who have I got to work with? What equipment do the Commandos have? Do I need to find more equipment to achieve the specified mission objectives? Unfortunately, the answer to the last question is always "yes". The Generals may tell you to blow up gun emplacements, but they rarely issue you the explosives to do it.

PLAN "B"

It's important to realize that there's more than one way to achieve the mission objectives in *Commandos 2*. There are efficient ways, stealthy ways, and bloody ways. But there is no one *right* way. Plan "B" isn't a single, magic alternative. It's a willingness to look at other options and different routes to your targets. It's making certain that you're not making a simple task overly complicated. And while making the most of your Commando's talents is vital during a mission, remembering

There's no single right way to complete a mission in COMMANDOS 2. It's good to have alternatives.

to regularly Quicksave your game is arguably much more important. Some of the missions in *Commandos 2* can take hours to play and finish.

KNOW YOUR ENEMY

Commandos 2 features German and Japanese armed units, and it's important to take some time to familiarize yourself with them. In both armies, there are three distinct ranks of fighting man—soldiers (armed with Rifles or Machineguns), Lieutenants (carrying Pistols), and Officers (also equipped with Pistols). In addition to these basic unit types, there are several *special* units to be wary of. These include:

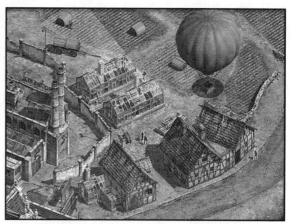

Patience is the key to successfully completing the missions in COMMANDOS 2. Watch the enemy and learn.

- **Civilians:** Includes sailors, technicians, mechanics, and workers. They're mostly unarmed, but can still raise the alarm if they spot you.

- **Snipers:** Like your own Sniper, these sharpshooter units can be deadly, picking off your Commandos from long range with a single shot. Snipers can be identified by their lighter-colored combat fatigues.
- **Grenadiers:** Just when you thought you could creep up behind any soldier and stab him to death, some soldiers respond with Grenades. Use the Binoculars to identify them.
- **Divers:** Providing a threat to your Diver while he's underwater, enemy divers are also armed with Harpoon Guns, which can kill your Commando outright with one well-aimed shot. There are usually several of them in the water at once, so be careful.
- **Spotters:** These soldiers carry Binoculars so that they have a much greater range of vision. If they spot you, they'll call in gunnery support or other soldiers to do their dirty work.
- **Heavy Machinegunners:** If you manage to wipe out the Heavy Machinegunners, you can take control of their machine guns for your own use.
- **Patrols:** Typically consists of groups of five enemies: a Lieutenant or Officer, plus four soldiers. They follow a pre-set patrol route.

COMBAT TRAINING

The terrain varies from mission to mission and objectives change, but one thing in *Commandos 2* remains constant. In each mission you must know how to dispatch enemy soldiers efficiently and without injuring your own troops in the process. Often, you must do this quietly, remaining undetected. A lone Commando can easily fight one soldier at a time. But he'll struggle to fight 20 of them if an alarm is raised, especially if they're all armed with Rifles and Machineguns. With this in mind, your weapons of choice should be the Knife (carried by the Diver and the Green Beret) and your fists.

The enemy can be alerted to your presence in several ways. First, they can *hear* you—you'll attract their attention if you fire a gun, detonate an explosive, or even run within earshot. Second, they can *see* you—each soldier has a Field of Vision and if you stray into it, you'll be spotted, identified, and shot (unless disguised). Also, the enemies will know someone is sneaking around if alarms sound, guards shout warnings, or guard dogs bark like crazy.

Whichever enemy units you encounter, make sure that you can kill them or knock them out (and remove the body) without attracting the attention of their trigger-happy comrades. In this section, our Drill Sergeant takes you through the basics of Commando Combat.

DOES YOUR TARGET MOVE?

Once you've identified a soldier that you want to "remove," be careful not to go blundering in with a Knife as soon as his back is turned. Make sure you have a safe hiding place and watch to see if your target moves. In *Commandos 2*, some soldiers guard specific locations, while others patrol between several of them in a predictable, looping route. Once you know if your target moves and where he moves to, you can start planning the next phase of your attack.

Study your target before you strike. Note if the target moves and where it moves to.

WHAT CAN THE TARGET SEE?

Select the Field of Vision icon on the Commando sidebar (or press [Tab]) and click on the target soldier. This shows you where the soldier is looking and how far he can see. If the target's Field of Vision is green, he is currently unaware of any threats. If it's red, he has been alerted to a potential danger and is actively searching for intruders. If you stray into his line of sight, he'll immediately identify you as hostile. A red Field of Vision will change back to green in time—simply wait. Once you know where your target is looking, you'll know whether you can sneak up on him unnoticed.

Use the Field of Vision icon to see where your target looks. Can you sneak up behind him? Or do you need to lure him away?

WHO CAN SEE YOUR TARGET?

Before you strike, find out if any other soldiers will spot you when you attack. You can use F11 to highlight nearby enemies, or select the Field of Vision icon again (Tab) and click the cursor on the ground near the target. This generates a red "X" called a View Marker. If another soldier can see this View Marker, his Field of Vision will be displayed, alerting you to his presence and position. Only attack when you are satisfied that nobody will see you approach your target, or that you can time your mugging when other nearby soldiers are looking away.

Make sure that other soldiers don't spot you killing one of their comrades.

WHO SHOULD ATTACK YOUR TARGET?

You know *who* you want to attack. You have watched *how* they move. You know *where* they look. The Green Beret and Diver are both highly skilled with the Knife. Stabbing a soldier from behind is a quick and easy way to dispatch them. Although the Diver can hit targets from some distance, this benefit is balanced by the fact that he must retrieve his thrown Knife *and* pick up the body. The Green Beret has no such problem. Other Commandos must resort to the Stun attack after which they must tie and gag the victim (except the Thief).

The Green Beret and the Diver can use the Knife to quiet and deadly effect. Punching guards is equally effective.

THE ART OF DISTRACTION

In most cases, your Commandos won't be able to simply sneak up behind an enemy to kill them or knock them out. The majority need to be "lured" away from their guard posts or patrol routes. The enemies will do anything for a free pack of Cigarettes or Wine Bottle. Throwing either of these handy distractions into an enemy's cone-shaped Field of Vision generally causes him to abandon his position and retrieve your gift. This method is vital for maneuvering enemy troops into a place where an attack is easier and safer to attempt.

The German and Japanese soldiers will usually do anything to get a free pack of Cigarettes or a Wine Bottle.

The main distractions in *Commandos 2* are the Cigarettes and the Wine Bottles—don't be without at least one of each. You can add the Decoy to this list, but, unlike the Cigarettes and Wine Bottle, this needs to be placed rather than thrown. Other temporary distractions include the Thief's trick-performing rat (Spike); Whiskey, the amazing item-carrying dog; and Wilson, the shaggy-haired sailor. More permanent forms of distraction can be provided by the skills of the Spy and flirtatious nature of part-time Commando Natasha.

ONE-MAN DISTRACT AND DISABLE

The one-man Distract and Disable technique relies mostly on Cigarettes, which can be guaranteed to spark the attention of low-ranking enemies. For Officers, the Wine Bottle is a more effective lure. The idea is simple—make your target move away from his position so a Commando can attack him from the rear or side.

Use a distraction like Cigarettes to lure an enemy guard away from his assigned patrol route or position.

Use the Field of Vision display to check where your target looks, and make sure that you throw the Cigarettes or Wine Bottle where only one target can see it. You don't want to draw more than one enemy toward you at a time. You can use several packs of Cigarettes in a "trail" to guide an enemy to a more convenient position.

TWO-MAN DISTRACT AND DISABLE

The two-man Distract and Disable relies not on a distracting object, but a distracting person. Use the Spy or Natasha to make an enemy soldier look away or turn his back to you. This leaves you clear to sneak up behind him to kill or knock him out. The Spy's Distract skill has two further options—he can get an enemy of lower rank to look in another direction or to move a short distance in a specified direction. This allows you more flexibility to position the targeted soldier for an attack.

Use the Spy or Natasha to distract an enemy guard, allowing your Commandos to sneak up behind them unnoticed.

ATTACKING BUILDINGS

During most missions, you'll have to survey and storm enemy buildings. As a general rule, always look before you leap. Use the Examine icon at the bottom of the sidebar (or W) to either look through a door or window, or up and down a ladder. Doing so allows you to see the inside of the room and to note the movements and positions of any enemies before you strike. Successful room clearance depends on the number of enemies, their positions, and the weapons they're carrying. Unarmed

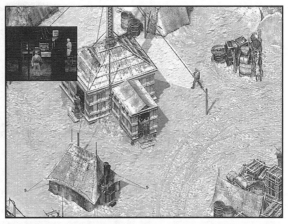

Use W to look through doors or windows, and up and down ladders before you use them.

targets will fight heroically (but poorly) with their fists. Use natural cover to divide and conquer your opponents.

CLEANING UP

It's vital to the success of any mission that you clean up any military mess you make. Specifically, this means moving the bodies of any soldiers that you kill or knock out. Leaving dead or unconscious soldiers lying in plain view will likely attract the attention of their comrades. Admittedly, there are times when this sort of distraction can helpfully lure guards out of position. But generally, take the time to carry enemy bodies to places where they won't be seen. Behind or inside cleared buildings is the safest option. Finally, don't forget to search each enemy you dispatch for extra equipment, weaponry, and ammunition.

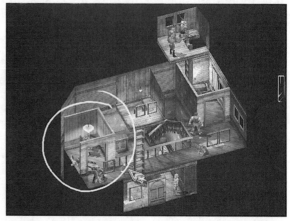

If you don't hide the bodies of dead or knocked out soldiers, they'll be spotted by their comrades and the alarm will be raised.

OTHER TACTICS

- **Defuse and Reuse:** The Sapper can not only locate and defuse Mines and Anti-Tank Mines, once they're disabled he also can pick them up, store them, and reuse them later in the mission.

- **Standing Coverage:** This auto-fire option allows you to preset a cone-shaped area of fire for a Commando. Select a weapon (such as a Rifle or Machinegun) and click the Standing Coverage icon on the sidebar (or hit ⓧ).

Be aware of the full array of talents that each Commando possesses. There's more to them than shoot and stab.

- **Barrels:** These heavy drums explode when hit by a bullet. Only the Green Beret is strong enough to move them. To take out a large group of soldiers, plant a Mine and positioning Barrels so they'll detonate in the blast.

- **Pitfalls:** The Driver can use his Shovel to dig small, deep holes. Place a packet of Cigarettes beyond the hole to lure enemy soldiers. As they move toward the cigarettes, they'll clumsily fall into it.

- **Bottle It:** Natasha can incapacitate enemy soldiers by hitting them over the head with a Wine Bottle.

- **Hit, Tie, and Gag:** Hold [Shift] to tie up unconscious enemy soldiers. They'll remain tied until one of their fellow soldiers frees them.

TRAINING MISSIONS

CHAPTER 5

TRAINING CAMP 1

PRIMARY OBJECTIVES

- Neutralize all the enemies at the border gate
- Get to the guard post
- Get the Wirecutters from the metal box
- Cut through the barbed wire and deactivate the Mines
- Fight the Officer groups

SECONDARY OBJECTIVE

- Obtain the contents of the wooden box

WALKTHROUGH

This is a small area, packed with enemy soldiers. Nevertheless, this compact scenario provides a good test of the combat skills that your Commandos will need later in the game. The landscape features patrolling guards, sentries, barbed wire fences, and hidden Mines. Try zooming out the camera view ([−]) to get a feel for the layout of the enemy checkpoint. You start this particular mission with the Thief and the Sapper.

Use the Sapper to knock out (⟨Q⟩) and tie up (⟨Shift⟩) the sentry next to your start point. Do this when the patrolling German soldier is walking away from this sentry toward the large bunker. Pick up and carry the knocked out sentry behind the bushes before the patrolling guard returns. Search the sentry and relieve him of his Cigarettes and his Rifle.

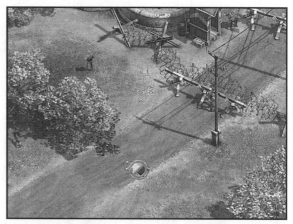

Controlling the Sapper, sneak up behind the nearest guard and knock him out. Carry the body away before the patrolling guard returns.

Attract the attention of the next guard by using Cigarettes to lure him away from his patrol route.

Next, throw the Cigarettes onto the road to entice the patrolling guard closer to your hiding place. Sneak out from behind the bushes and knock out this second soldier. Tie him up and gag him (⟨Shift⟩) and carry the body out of sight. Search the captured guard to get another Rifle and retrieve the pack of Cigarettes if you haven't already done so. Finally, using the Sapper again, walk up behind the soldier working at the red-and-white barrier. Knock him out, tie and gag him, and dump the body behind the bushes.

Now take control of the Thief. Move the Thief to the nearby telephone pole and, using the [Shift] key, left-click on the pole to make the Thief climb it. Guide the Thief across the telephone wires to the telephone pole directly in front of the small semicircular bunker. Climb down and crawl around the bunker to the metal crate to unlock it. Inside the box, you'll find a pair of Wirecutters and two Grenades. Climb the telephone pole again and go hand-over-hand back across the wires. Move the Thief back toward the starting position. Give the Grenades and the Wirecutters to the Sapper.

To reach the far bunker and the metal crate there, use the Thief's skill at climbing telephone poles.

Take care of the soldier hiding behind the bushes before you cut the barbed wire and move through.

Next, crawl in front of the barbed-wire fencing to the right of the screen (as viewed in the pictures here). Crawl around behind the soldier in the bushes. Use the Sapper to knock out the guard and to tie him up and gag him. Search the unconscious soldier for more Cigarettes and a Machinegun.

Still controlling the Sapper, crawl back along the barbed wire fence until you're within Grenade range of the large bunker. Use Ⓐ to throw a Grenade into the bunker, killing the guards there. The explosion will attract the attention of the remaining guards, who'll begin a half-hearted search of the area. While the enemy panics, crawl back along the barbed wire fence to a position that is as far away from the guard hut as possible.

Kill the group of soldiers in the large bunker using one of the Grenades you pilfered earlier from the metal crate.

Cut through the barbed wire fence and defuse the Mines that are buried beyond it. You can pick up the Mines and reuse them.

Monitor the vision of the guard at the hut (Tab) and cut through the barbed wire fence where he can't spot you. Be cautious—there are Mines buried in the ground beyond the wire. Use the Sapper and his Mine Detector to locate and defuse the hidden explosives. Pick up one of the recently disabled Mines, crawl past the vision cone of the guard at the hut, and plant the explosive at the end of the second red-and-white barrier. This deals with the guard in the second bunker when you kill the guard at the hut.

Crawl back to a firing position next to the telephone pole opposite the guard hut. Shoot the guard there using one of the Rifles you picked up earlier. Immediately start crawling back toward the hole in the wire. When the final guard comes to check

on you, he'll set off the Mine you planted earlier. When there are no more threats, examine the wooden box next to the guard hut to find a First Aid Kit. Check the Notebook to make sure that you have completed all the required mission objectives.

Shoot the soldier at the guard hut using the Rifle. The gunshot alerts the remaining soldier, who comes to investigate.

TRAINING CAMP 2

PRIMARY OBJECTIVES

- Rescue the Allied soldiers who have split from their unit
- Obtain the key to the house
- Contact your allies
- Use the enemy radio to contact HQ
- Fight the Officer groups

SECONDARY OBJECTIVE

- Obtain the contents of the wooden boxes
- Defend against the enemy attack
- Destroy the enemy tank

WALKTHROUGH

Set during a gun battle between Allied and German soldiers, this second training scenario requires you to kill or disable all the enemy troops. You have been given three Commandos to control in this mission—the Green Beret, the Sapper, and the Driver.

From the start position, use the Sapper and his Cigarettes to lure away the German

Start by clearing out all the soldiers on this lower level. As usual, packs of Cigarettes work wonders.

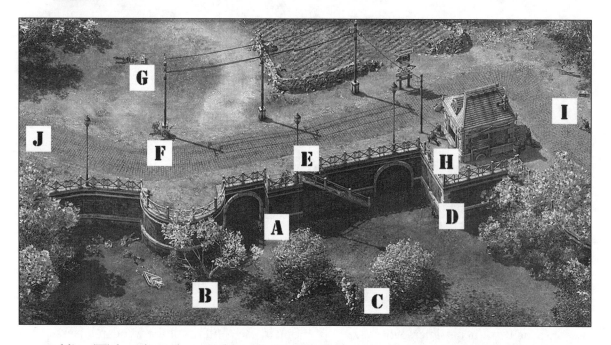

soldier (**A**) kneeling close to the wall. When he's close enough, knock him out, then tie him up and gag him. Search the captured guard to get a Rifle. Next use the Green Beret to knife the nearby soldier (**B**) in the trees—make sure you do this when the Officer (**D**) at the far end of this area is talking to his Lieutenant.

Next, take control of the Green Beret and crawl toward the soldier (**C**) kneeling next to the semicircular wall. None of the other soldiers will see you approach. Again, knife this soldier when the Officer (**D**) talks to his Lieutenant. Drag the body out of sight (behind the nearest tree is perfect). Search the soldier's body (**C**) to get a Machinegun.

Move the Green Beret along the bottom of the screen and stab the soldier kneeling next to the semicircular wall.

Several Germans remain on this ground level—two riflemen on the stairs at position **E** and an Officer (**D**) who seems to be directing the battle above. The Officer receives regular reports from a Lieutenant in the field. Move the Green Beret to stand behind the wall near the German Officer. The best time to knife the Officer is when he kneels down after his chat with the Lieutenant. You should have enough time to attack him, pick up the body, and take it behind the wall. Search the dead Officer to find a set of keys. These open the building on the street above.

Monitor the vision of the Officer and move behind the wall when he's not looking.

Pick off the guards on the stairway. This is the only route up to the street level.

The only way up to the street is via the stairs. But these are occupied by the Lieutenant and two riflemen. Watch how these soldiers move. The Lieutenant and one of the riflemen remain stationary, while the third soldier regularly crawls up and down the steps. Using one of the Rifles that you've stolen, shoot the crawling soldier when he reaches the bottom of the steps. Shoot the Lieutenant when he comes down to examine the body of his dead comrade. Finally, crawl up the steps and shoot the last rifleman. Search the bodies to find more ammunition or weaponry.

Making sure one of your Commandos is holding some Cigarettes (and a Rifle), move him to the top of the steps. Watch the two soldiers near the telephone pole at position (**F**). One soldier stays put while the other crawls back and forth to position (**G**) near the wooden box. Lure the crawling soldier toward your position on the steps using the Cigarettes. Shoot him with the Rifle when he's in range. Next, crawl forward and pick off the soldier next to the telephone pole at (**F**). Then creep forward and shoot the soldier next to the wooden box at (**G**). Search the bodies for ammunition. Open the wooden box to find a First Aid Kit and two cans of Food.

Aid the beleaguered Allied troops by shooting the three German soldiers who are attacking them from this side of the map.

Once the left side of the map is clear, turn your attention to the soldiers defending the building.

Next, take out the soldiers surrounding the building. Pick off the guard (**H**) using a Rifle. If you keep close to the railings as you approach him, he won't see you. Stay in that position and shoot the other soldier who joins him. Search both bodies to stock up on ammunition. Look through the window of the building (**W**) to see the guards inside. Bring up the Driver and throw a Molotov Cocktail through the window to take them out. If one escapes out the door, the Allied soldiers should get him.

Now there should be five enemy soldiers left, all located near the road (**I**) on the other side of the building. Make sure that the Green Beret has a Rifle with at least three bullets and crawl around the back of the building. Shoot the guard across the road first, then sneak up and stab the one kneeling next to the barrels. Use the Rifle again to pick off the two soldiers across the road near the box before creeping up behind the final guard with a Knife. Search the box here to find Grenades, Molotov Cocktails, and Smoke Grenades.

Using the Green Beret, crawl around the back of the building to attack the remaining soldiers from behind.

Use the Standing Coverage command to order your troops to fire at anybody who comes down the road.

NOTE

Press ⎣Spacebar⎦ to have your Commandos stand or lay down, then use ⎣x⎦ to provide coverage.

Move one of your Commandos into the building and use the radio—you'll need the Officer's keys to open the door. When you've done this, an icon appears on the bottom-right of the screen that indicates a German counteroffensive. The attack itself will come along the road from **J**. Get the Anti-Tank Mines from the box here. Now move some of the Allied riflemen to cover the roadway, using the Ground Coverage (⎣X⎦) option. Support the riflemen by setting the Green Beret to provide Standing Coverage fire (⎣X⎦) with a Machinegun or Rifle. Use the Sapper to plant an Anti-Tank Mine in the middle of the road. As soon as you click the icon, the German reinforcements begin to arrive. Your troops should be able to pick them off before they advance down the road. The mine will take care of the tank that follows.

COMBAT MISSIONS

CHAPTER 6

NIGHT OF THE WOLVES

PRIMARY OBJECTIVES

- Contact Natasha
- Steal the Enigma machine from the General's safe
- Contact the wounded ally
- Steal the office key from the General's assistant
- Decipher messages with the Enigma machine
- Use the radio

SECONDARY OBJECTIVES

- Use Sleeping Pills to knock out the General's assistant
- Have Natasha call the General
- Disconnect power to the electric fence
- Steal the ID Documents

WALKTHROUGH

There are no simple missions in *Commandos 2*. The first scenario makes things difficult from the start—infiltrate a heavily guarded enemy base using a single unarmed Commando. You start with the Thief, but make contact with resistance beauty Natasha along the way.

Jump out of the boat ([X]) and approach the enemy base via its least-defended area—the large docks ([A]). Monitor the vision of the soldier guarding this area and swim slowly to the steps near the dock. Lie on the metal grating below the surface of the water and next to the steps. Throw the Thief's Cigarettes to lure the guard into the corner, giving you time to sneak up behind him to perform a Stun attack ([Q]). The Thief can't tie up and gag unconscious soldiers. So quickly climb the wall ([B]) to the roof before the guard recovers.

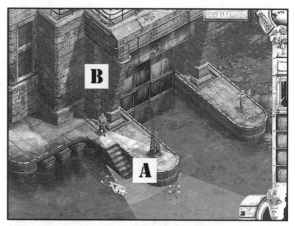

Leave the boat and swim slowly toward the dock area.

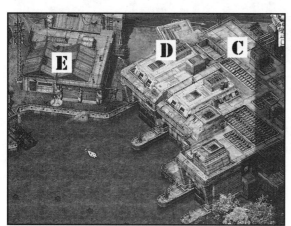

After you've made it to the roof, work your way to the building where Natasha is located.

Go across the roof, avoiding the patrolling guards. Move to position ([C]), and use the ladder ([D]) to get to ground level. Sneak to the stairway that leads to the roof of the nearby building ([E]). Inside this building is where you'll find your resistance contact, Natasha.

There's no way you can enter the building from the side—you need to enter via the front door. Crawl up the stairway and wait until both patrolling guards on the roof are standing together. When they both turn to move away, click on the sloping roof to move the Thief there. Keeping low, crawl toward the corner of the roof where a third guard stands watch.

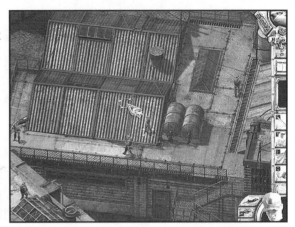

Quicksave your game before attempting to sneak past the guards and onto the sloping roof here.

It's a bold Commando who enters an enemy stronghold via the front door. You will be that bold Commando....

Crawl past the stationary guard when the patrolling guards can't spot you and make your way to the corner of the roof. Climb down the wall behind the two men talking on the pier. There's another patrolling guard here, too, so make sure you aren't spotted. Finally, crawl along the ground toward the door and enter the building.

Inside the building, wait until the technician (**F**) goes to examine the nearby crates (these are directly opposite the room where Natasha is located). Using the pack of Cigarettes, distract the soldier, and knock him out. Walk into Natasha's room before the technician turns around. Move the mouse pointer over Natasha, hold down Shift and left-click to talk to her. Quickly hide behind the table in this room so you're not spotted when the guard recovers and searches the area.

The Thief can knock out enemy soldiers, but he CAN'T tie them up and gag them.

After you talk to Natasha and gain control of her, use her to distract the technician (⑤). Once the technician is transfixed, move the Thief out of the building, knocking out the soldier along the way as you did before. Once outside, move the Thief to a safe hiding place on the roof and leave him there. Take control of Natasha again for the next part of the mission.

Like the Spy, Natasha possesses the ability to distract enemy guards. She does this with lipstick, a short skirt, and a pout.

Natasha's disguise will fool most enemy soldiers, but high-ranking Officers will recognize her as a traitor.

Natasha can walk around the base freely if she doesn't act suspiciously. High-ranking soldiers will recognize her, so keep your distance if you see any. In the room where you found her, check the locker to find a First Aid Kit and some Cigarettes, plus a piece of the **bonus** photograph. Search the shelves in the main room to get some Sleeping Pills. Locate the power room for the electric fencing. Throw the switch next to the locked doors while the technician isn't looking. The other switch turns all the floodlights off—throw this one, too.

Guide Natasha out of the building (using the same route as the Thief) and into the building next to it—the building that has "A-2" painted on the roof. Talk to the wounded ally here to receive a Whistle and an Encrypted Message. You need to decipher the two messages you have with the Enigma machine. You also gain Whiskey. Whiskey is an incredibly useful advantage on this level, allowing you to send items between the characters quickly and easily.

The wounded ally is in the nearby building. Look for "A-2" painted on the roof in big lettering.

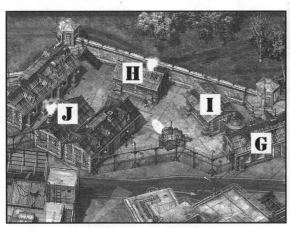

Zoom out the camera view (−) and locate the General's office in the compound farthest from the sea.

The next part of the mission is to retrieve the Enigma machine from a heavily protected compound (to check the map, hit F9). It's a barracks area, so it's crammed with enemy soldiers. Avoid any high-ranking troops and move Natasha to the roof where the Thief is hiding. Provide enough distraction so that the Thief can get off of the roof via the stairway. Move the Thief and Natasha to the shower block (G). The Enigma machine is in the General's office (H). The door, however, is locked and requires a key. You'll need to get the key from the General's assistant in building I.

Controlling the Thief, look through the window of the shower block and watch the movement of the single guard inside. When he goes into the shower, move the Thief through one of the windows. Search the cabinet for another **bonus** photo piece. Move out through the door into the compound before you are spotted. Natasha can make her own way to this position using the door.

Enter the compound by sneaking through the window of the shower block. Careful—there's a guard endlessly washing inside.

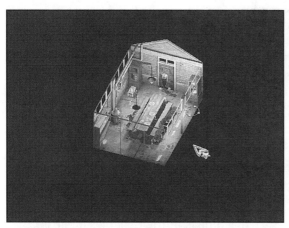

To open the door to the General's office, you need the key from the General's assistant in building **I**.

Move Natasha into the barracks area (**I**). It's right next to the shower block. Here you'll find the General's assistant and several others eating and drinking. Examine the crate on the floor in the corner of the room—it's full of Wine. Use the Sleeping Pills on the Wine and exit the inventory. Wait until the men drink the Poisoned Wine and fall asleep. Press W to have Natasha search the unconscious men—the General's assistant is the man in the gray shirt, nearest the door. Take the keys from him. Search one of the cupboards in the corner for another **bonus** photo piece before leaving.

Move Natasha up to the General's office (**H**) and unlock the door. The General needs to be distracted before you can get to the safe in the corner of his room. First of all, however, you need to move the Thief to a position outside the office. Use Natasha's skills to distract the guard wandering around the compound with a flashlight. Move the Thief behind the distracted guard and into a hiding place between the General's office and the wall. Hold down (Shift) and click on the gap to hide there.

The Thief can hide in the gaps between the buildings in this compound. Hold down (Shift) and left-click on a suitable gap.

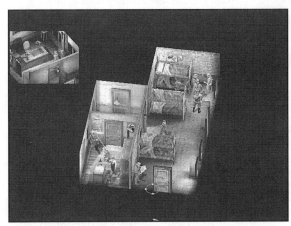

Before you can get to the safe, distract the General and lure him out of his office.

Now move Natasha down the narrow passageway and into the door of building **J** (see previous screenshot). Hold the mouse pointer over the phone and press (Shift) to telephone the General. Quickly switch back to the Thief and wait until the General leaves his office. Left-click to leave the hiding place and enter the office. Knock out the enemy soldier here, and open the safe with the Lockpick. Get the Enigma machine and the ID Documents. Leave the office before the KO'd soldier wakes up or the General returns. Hide the Thief in the corner again.

Decode the Encrypted Message using the Enigma machine. When you've done this, another objective appears—you must use the radio to tell the Allies that the Germans have captured a submarine. Send Natasha to the radio room (**K**)—she needs the assistant's keys to get there via the small door next to the larger gates.

The Germans have captured an Allied submarine they are keeping in the large building. Retrieving it is your next mission.

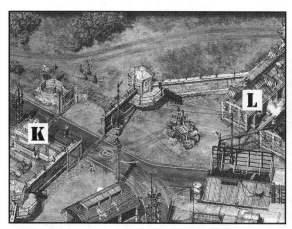

Send Natasha to the radio room on the edge of the base. Use the radio to receive the last mission objective.

Use the radio inside building **K** to receive the final objective. The Thief is ordered to hide pending a further mission. The building that has been chosen (**L**) is fortunately very close to the General's office. The last two pieces of the **bonus** photograph are in the barracks area, next to the telephone Natasha used to contact the General. Use Natasha to search the lockers and find them. When done, climb in through the window of the building and hide under the bunks here to finish the Night of the Wolves mission.

Hide the Thief under the bed in this room. He'll still be here when you start the next mission—Das Boot.

MISSION SECRET

Bonus photo pieces required: 5

This bonus mission uses the same landscape as the first tutorial mission. You are ordered to eliminate all enemy soldiers, find the Mine Detector, deactivate the Mines, and escape in the enemy vehicle. Like the tutorial mission, you command the Sapper and the Thief.

Start by neutralizing the soldier near the Sapper and the patrolling soldier who paces back-and-forth nearby. Knock out and tie them both up. Shoot the soldier next to the guard hut using a Rifle. This will attract the attention of the soldier standing next to the car. Shoot this soldier once he's within range. Move the Thief over the telephone wires towards the far bunker. Unlock and open the nearby metal crate to get the Mine Detector and

Wirecutters. Knock out the guard in the bunker and open the second metal crate to get Grenades and a Timed Bomb. Send the Thief back to the Sapper.

Give the Grenades, Mine Detector, and Timed Bomb to the Sapper. Move the Sapper within range of the patrolling guard beyond the guard hut. Throw one Grenade to take them all out, then a second Grenade to kill the final guard who runs to investigate. Use the Wirecutters to cut through the fence, locate and defuse all of the Mines (there are five), then escape in the car.

You need to deactivate ALL of the Mines to complete the bonus mission objective. There are five of them.

CHAPTER 7

DAS BOOT, SILENT KILLERS

PRIMARY OBJECTIVES

- Rescue all the Allied sailors
- Find the prison key
- Deactivate the underwater Mines
- Open the hangar door
- Escape in the submarine

SECONDARY OBJECTIVES

- Cut the barbed wire and deactivate Mines
- Pass the Security Papers to the Spy via Whiskey
- Enter the base disguised as an official
- Steal a vehicle
- Call the Green Beret using the radio
- Rescue the Captain
- Destroy the torpedoes
- Find the Enigma codes
- Destroy the AA Guns
- Blow up the gas tanks

WALKTHROUGH

In this mission, you have control of the Diver, the Sapper, the Spy, and the Thief. The Commandos are split into two groups—the first three start in a boat offshore while the Thief remains hidden under the bunks where you left him at the end of the Night of the Wolves mission. For most of the mission, you control the Sapper, Diver, and Spy. Whiskey is also available and any of the four Commandos can summon him.

Send the Diver, Sapper, and Spy into the water. Swim them toward the landing area, taking note of where the solitary guard is looking—he slowly covers a 180-degree arc, so you can swim past when he's looking toward the rest of the base. Send the Sapper to knock out the guard. Tie him up and steal his uniform and Rifle. Bring the rest of the team ashore.

Swim up to the landing area right of the docks. Move slowly so the nearby sentry doesn't spot you.

Watch out for the Mines buried behind the first barbed wire fence and in front of the second one.

Using the Sapper's Wirecutters, snip through the first barbed wire fence. Before you go through, press D to detect the Mines that are hidden beyond it. There are four explosive charges arranged in a line across the section of fence you cut.

Defuse the Mines and move on up the pathway. Pan the view to the technician working on a metal walkway in the facility beyond the wall. He'll spot you as you approach, as you'll be waving about a Mine Detector.

Monitor the vision of the technician and activate the Sapper's Mine Detector. There are two rows of Mines hidden before the second barbed wire fence. Be careful when you're working in the middle of the path.

The technician might spot you, and there's also a German Officer who's smoking in front of the compound. Wait, and he'll move from a position under the tree to walk in front of the guard tower, to the truck, and back again. Monitor his vision to see when you can safely defuse the Mines and cut through the second fence.

A patrolling Officer makes defusing the second set of Mines difficult. Make sure he doesn't spot you.

After the Spy has stolen an Officer's uniform, he can distract lower-ranking Lieutenants and soldiers.

Sneak up to stand close to the guard tower. Lure the patrolling Officer away with some Cigarettes (the Diver has some). Knock out the Officer and tie him up. Steal his Cigarettes and uniform. Give the Officer's uniform to the Spy.

Now use the Spy (dressed in the Officer's uniform) to distract the soldier patrolling outside the gate. Make him look away from the gates. Lure away the soldier standing in front of the gates and knock him out or kill him. Dump the body before returning to knock out and tie up the soldier who's still talking to the Spy.

Use this spare moment to select the Thief. Transfer the Security Papers from the last mission to Whiskey. Get the Spy or another character to summon the dog with the Whistle. (The Thief may have to open the door to let him out.) When the dog arrives, give the Security Papers to the Spy to complete one of the mini-mission objectives. Now zoom out the view (⊟) and study the layout of the base beyond the large gates.

Apart from the Spy dressed in the Officer's uniform, don't send anybody else into the base yet. Distract soldier Ⓐ on the raised platform—keep him looking away from the gates. Sneak in your Sapper while soldiers Ⓑ and Ⓒ aren't looking. Hide him around the back of the yellow tanks at Ⓓ.

Let soldier Ⓑ spot the Sapper. Knock him out when he runs to investigate. Move the Spy to distract soldier Ⓒ. Make him face away from soldier Ⓐ, and use the Sapper to knock out soldier Ⓐ.

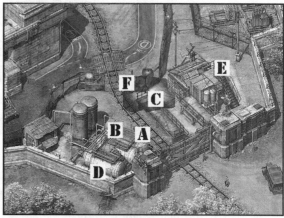

Five enemy soldiers—Ⓐ, Ⓑ, Ⓒ, Ⓔ and Ⓕ—are stationed in this part of the base. Take them out quietly so you don't set off the alarm.

Soldier Ⓔ, standing on the balcony, is a Sniper. If you don't kill him now, he'll prove troublesome later.

Send the Diver to kill soldier Ⓒ with his throwing Knife. Hide the body. Clear the rest of this area. Take out the Sniper (Ⓔ) on the balcony near the electrical station. Do this by hiding the Diver under the stairs, then using the Spy to talk to the Sniper.

Press Ⓢ to distract the sniper, then press Ⓔ to direct him down the steps—if you knock out the sniper on the balcony, soldiers beyond the wall will spot you. When the Sniper gets to the bottom of the stairs, kill him with a throwing Knife.

There's only one more guard in this area (**F**), and he blocks the way to the large building—the submarine pen. Lure him out of position with Cigarettes and distract him (**S**) with the Spy. Using another Commando, creep up behind him and knock him out.

Send the Spy up the railroad track to where two more German soldiers are talking. Distract them so they look away from the gates. Send the Sapper and the Diver crawling toward the gates, then to the side of the large building. If you don't crawl here, you'll be spotted and the alarm will sound.

Use the Spy's talents to distract the guard looking down the railroad track. Move your Sapper and Diver to the edge of the submarine pen.

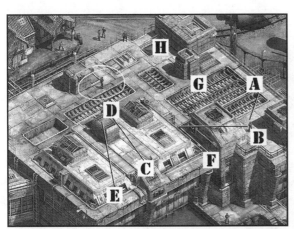

The best way into the submarine pen is via the door at **H**. But you need to take out all of the guards and the patrolling Lieutenant to make it.

To rescue the trapped sub crew, you need to unlock their prison cell. A high-ranking German walking on the roof of the submarine pen has the all-important key. There are eight enemies stationed on the roof. Check their positions by zooming out the game view (**-**).

Send the Spy up via the metal staircase and use him to distract the guard (**B**) patrolling nearby—make him face away from the staircase and the nearby ladder. Monitor the vision of the key-holding Lieutenant—he walks a long path across the roof and is dressed in gray. When he turns away, send the Diver up the ladder and kill the guard (**A**). Move his body before the Lieutenant returns. Next, knife soldier **B**, whom the Spy is still distracting.

Turn your attention to guards C, D, and E. There's a path leading to a ledge at the front of the building, allowing you to sneak up on the guard with his back to the sea (C). Use the Diver to knife him. Send the Diver along the path, up a small set of steps, and onto the roof to retrieve his weapon.

The guard on the opposite side (D) has his back to you. Sneak up when the Lieutenant isn't looking. Knife him and hide the body. Deal with the last soldier (E) on the edge of the building. This guy is a Sniper, but he's facing the sea, so the Diver can easily knife him. Get the Spy to retrieve the Knife—there's an eagle-eyed guard on the nearby roof.

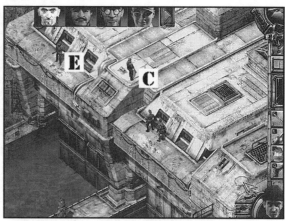

Kill the Sniper at E. If you don't, he'll target your men when they swim across the water later in the mission.

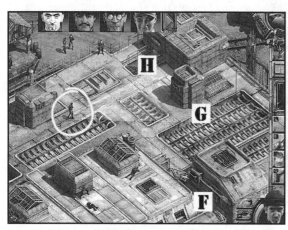

Lure the Lieutenant (circled) into the passageway at F. He has the key to free the submarine crew.

One of the two remaining guards has his back to you. The other is an Officer near H who will see through your disguise if you get too close. To kill the Lieutenant and grab the keys, lure him into the small passageway you used earlier (F). Like most soldiers, he's a sucker for free Cigarettes. Use the Diver to knife him when he's close enough. Killing the Lieutenant at F ensures that he dies beyond the range of the remaining Officer.

Lure the last Officer away from H and kill him. Use G as a hiding place for this attack. You can now move all of your forces into the building. Send the Spy in first.

In the next room, kill or knock out the two technicians—they're unarmed. Send the Spy down the ladder and distract the sentry (**B**) walking along the edge of the submarine pen. Make sure he's facing away from soldier **A** by the ladder. Send down the Diver and lay him flat behind the crates. Attack soldier **A** and hide his body behind the crates.

Next, creep up behind the distracted guard (**B**) and kill him. Again hide the body. Be cautious here—you may have to deal with another soldier who follows you down the ladder. Be on the lookout for him and kill him quickly.

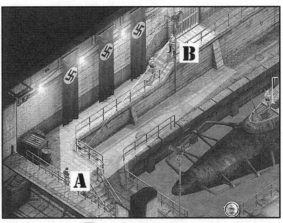

Distract guard **B** so you can safely knock out or kill the soldier at **A**. The Distract and Disable tactic works wonders in this section.

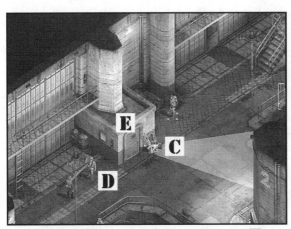

Distract guard **D** so you can safely kill soldier **C**. After you clear room **E**, you can use it to hide the bodies.

Maneuver the Spy so he distracts soldier **D** patrolling beyond the small room at **E**. When his back is turned to soldier **C**, use the Diver to creep up and kill soldier **C**. Hide soldier **C**'s body, then kill soldier **D**. Again, hide the body. Search the bodies of the guards to pick up Machineguns.

Look into small room **E**. Send in the Spy to distract the lone guard, then use the Diver to kill him. Search the wooden box here to find Grenades, explosives, and a Ladder. The switch here opens and closes the gates at the front of the base.

Leave E and note the guard on the steps watching over the empty dock. To successfully assassinate him, you must first distract the guard wandering along the second dock area (F). Use the Spy to turn the guard away from the soldier you want to kill, so the attack remains unseen. Take the body and hide it in E.

Distract the guard in the corner of the room at the end of the far dock. Turn him away from your soldiers and room E. When wandering guard F moves away, send in the Diver to kill the distracted guard. Remove the body before the wandering guard returns.

To protect your approach to the submarine, take out as many guards as you can.

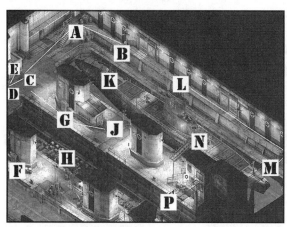

The area around the submarine is a daunting challenge. Take it one step at a time, one guard at a time.

Send the Spy back to the dock next to the submarine. Move the Spy along the side of the dock opposite the submarine via G, so you remain hidden from the guards on it.

NOTE
Enemies work in the dry dock below H, but their range of vision is limited.

Lure soldier I to point G using Cigarettes, then use the Spy to distract him so he turns his back to room E. Bring the Diver up (crawling) behind the distracted soldier (I) and stab him.

Dump the body in room E. Next, kill soldier J and unlock the door he was guarding with the key you took from the Lieutenant on the roof. Carry the body inside.

Inside is the crew of the captured sub. Hold down (Shift) and click on a crewman to untie him. Crawl the Diver toward room **E** via **G**. Stay low to avoid the gaze of soldier **H** in the dry dock.

You now need to get rid of soldiers **K**, **L**, and **M**. (See the earlier figure showing the area around the submarine.) Use the Diver to throw the knife and kill **K**—you can retrieve the Knife later. Send the Spy along the edge of the submarine to distract soldier **L**. Kill him silently from behind. Send the Spy to distract soldier **M**, who watches over the sub from a position above the dock gates. When his back is turned, he's easily killed.

Use the Diver to kill the soldier (**K**). Don't worry about losing the Knife, you can retrieve it later.

Hide the body of soldier **K** behind the sub's conning tower. If you don't, soldier **N** will spot it when you lure him out of position.

Monitor the vision of soldier **N**, who guards the gangplank on the deck of the sub. Control the Spy and move him onto the sub and down to the body of soldier **K**. Pick up the body and hide it behind the conning tower. Retrieve the Diver's Knife. Doing this allows you to lure soldier **N** onto the dock, ensuring that he isn't alerted to trouble by the dead body of a comrade. When the body has been moved, return to the dockside and attract the soldier (**N**) with a pack of Cigarettes. Distract him so either the Diver or Sapper can sneak up behind him.

All this work leaves the Lieutenant (**O**), who's guarding the door to the control room at the end of the dock. Lure him away from his position using Cigarettes, then use the Spy to distract him after he picks them up. Kill or knock out the Lieutenant.

Do the same for soldier **P** on the high platform. (See the figure showing the area around the submarine.) Lure him with Cigarettes, distract him when he picks them up, then use one of the other characters to attack from behind. This allows you to safely enter the door previously guarded by the Lieutenant (**O**).

Lure the Lieutenant (**O**) away from the building at the end of the dock using Cigarettes. Distract and then kill or knock him out.

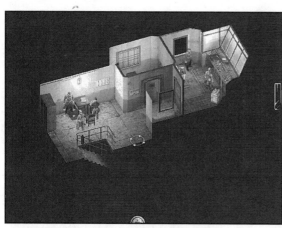

Use the Spy to distract any armed soldiers. Unarmed enemies will rarely raise the alarm and will ineffectually attack you with their fists.

In the room beyond, send the Spy to distract the Officer when he's close to the lockers at the end of the room. Send in one of the other characters to knock out and tie up the soldier sitting on the bench. Then knock out the distracted Officer.

Search the lockers to find Sleeping Pills, Wine, Grenades, another Knife, Poison, Binoculars, and a First Aid Kit. Next, send the Spy upstairs. Distract the soldier and turn him so his back is to the stairway. Bring up the Diver and punch the distracted soldier. This alerts the other soldier here. Quickly floor him with a punch. Tie up both men. Check the locker in the corner for more Wine, Binoculars, and a Ladder.

The submarine's Captain is being held in the next room. Unlock the door with the keys you found on the roof and free him. Clear out the men in the control room with a Grenade. Search the box to find the Enigma codes and activate the switch in the corner to open the gates of the submarine pen. Leave the building with the Captain.

Send the Spy into the sub via the forward hatch—the one closest to the gangplank. Distract the guard at the end of the first room, then send one of the other characters down the ladder to knock out the other guard. Kill the distracted guard.

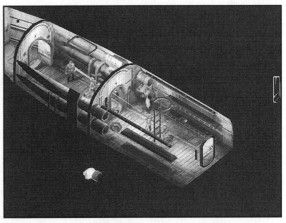

Use the Spy and the Diver to clear the submarine of enemy soldiers. Use the Two-Man Distract and Disable tactic (see Chapter 4).

The Diver needs to disable the underwater Mines so the sub can escape safely.

Work your way through the sub, distracting and disabling the enemy soldiers. When the lower level is clear, climb up to the conning tower, killing the guards there. Move the Captain and his crew aboard. Deactivate the underwater Mines outside and the sub will be ready to leave.

Equip the Diver's Diving Gear ([D]) and jump into the water. Swim through the open doors and into the sea beyond. Dive ([B]) and go to each of the six Mines in turn. Hold down [Shift] and click on each Mine to defuse it.

Now for the secondary objectives. Clear out the rest of the enemy soldiers in the submarine pen. Send the Spy into the dry dock via the ladder at **B**. Distract soldier **A** so he's not facing the other soldier working at the dock. Send the Diver or the Sapper to knock out and tie up the wandering worker. Afterward, knock out or kill the distracted guard. Return the way you came. Now turn your attention to guard **C**. Use the Spy to distract him at the end of his patrol route near point **D**, then knock out or kill him.

Follow the dock to get soldier **E**. Keep going to Distract and Disable soldier **F**. Double back and head for soldier **G**. Distract and Disable him. Wait until soldier **I** walks away from the building and the remaining guards at **H**.

Lure one of two guards away from **H** using Cigarettes and use the Spy to distract him when he picks them up. When soldier **I** isn't looking, knock out or kill the lured guard

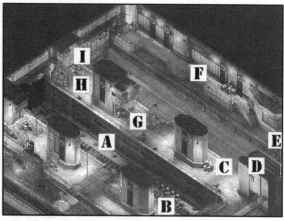

Clear out the other side of the submarine pen. You must be able to open the doors near the building at **I**.

and hide his body at point **G**. Lure soldier **I** down in the same way. The remaining guard at **H** should have his back to you and won't see your fist coming.

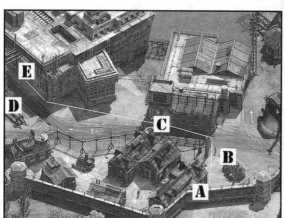

Move the Thief from **A**, behind the backs of the guards at **B**, to safe point **C**. When guard **D** is distracted, the Thief can make it to **E** to join the other Commandos.

NOTE

There are four bonus photo pieces found in the submarine pen. Two are located on the lover level of the submarine, while the other two are in the building at the end of the dock (next to the submarine).

The submarine pen is now clear. You've probably noticed lots of little metal boxes lying around—only the Thief can open them. To bring him over, send a German uniform to the Thief via Whiskey. Send the Spy to the Thief's location (A). Use the Spy to distract the soldier standing outside the Thief's door.

When the coast is clear, move the Thief (wearing the German uniform) through the door. Walk, don't run. Move the Spy outside. Use the Spy to distract the guard at B who's looking toward point C. This allows the Thief to move from A, behind the soldier at B, and to C without alerting any of the guards.

By the time you reach point C, the uniform will have been "used"—its effects are only temporary on most characters. Send another uniform to the Thief via Whiskey. Meanwhile, use the Spy to distract the guard at point D and make him look away from the double doors at E.

Move the Thief (wearing the fresh uniform) to point E and into the submarine pen. Unlock the various metal boxes to find a Bazooka, Flame Thrower, Grenades, and a Remote-Controlled Bomb.

You should remember this building from the previous mission. The torpedo you need to destroy is inside.

Send the Spy to open the other set of submarine pen doors—the switch is in the building at the end of the far dock. Next, send the Spy to deal with the two guards patrolling the front of the building where the torpedo is located. Lure the guard to the left of the building using Cigarettes. Place them in point A so you can avoid the gaze of other soldiers. After you lure the soldier away, knock him out using the Syringe—two doses ought to send him to the floor. Tie him up and use the Syringe on the other guard.

Now your team can swim out of the submarine pen doors and climb the steps at the front of the building. You won't get very far outside if you didn't deal with the Sniper on the roof earlier. (See the earlier figure showing the roof of the submarine pen.) If you didn't, go do it.

Send the Spy into the building first and Distract and Disable the first guard there. Use this tactic to get rid of the technicians. In most cases, even if one of the unarmed enemies here spots you, he won't raise the general alarm. There's a **bonus** photo piece in one of the cupboards here. Plant the Remote-Controlled Bomb you picked up earlier next to the torpedo and leave.

When you're in the submarine pen, detonate the torpedo charge. It destroys the torpedo and demolishes the entire building.

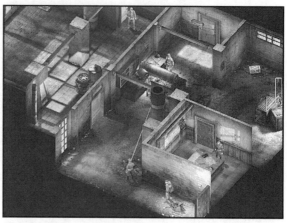

Use the Spy and the Sapper to Distract and Disable the soldier near the torpedo. Plant a Remote-Controlled Bomb next to it.

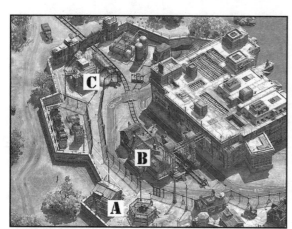

The switch at **A** turns the electric fencing off at the power station. More explosives are at **B** and **C**.

A little preparation is required for the remaining secondary objectives—the destruction of the yellow gas tanks and the three AA Guns. Take control of the Spy and visit locations **A**, **B**, and **C**. At **A**, enter the hut and turn off the electrified fencing—do this without being seen or you'll blow your cover.

Move to **B** and search the furniture to find a Remote-Controlled Bomb, Timed Bomb, and Grenades. The radio is also in this building. Use it discreetly. It allows you to specify a landing point for the Green Beret—he can parachute in if you need him. Find more explosives in the building at **C**.

Move the other squad members out through the submarine doors (next to the sub) and around through the entrance they used at the beginning of the mission. Make sure that you've already taken out the Sniper on the balcony—you're going to approach the first AA Gun via the power station. Cut the wire fence when the technician works on first right-hand generator. (See the preceding figure.) Walk to the technician and knock him out. Tie him up and search him to find another Remote-Controlled Bomb.

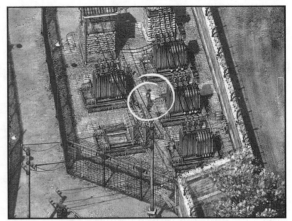

With the electricity turned off, approach the first AA Gun via the power station. Watch out for the technician.

Distract the guards near the power station and work your way to the first AA Gun. The soldier working on it won't see you approach.

Next, use the Spy to distract one of the two soldiers guarding the power station gate. Distract the one patrolling between the AA Gun and the electricity substations—make it close to the gun, with the soldier's back to the other sentry.

Move the Sapper through the substations and cut the wire behind the sentry outside the gate. Knock out the guard, tie him up, and carry away his body. Move the Sapper up to knock out the guard distracted by the Spy. Tie him up and carry away the body. Use the Spy to distract the soldier on the wall, and use the Sapper to plant a Remote-Controlled Bomb next to the AA Gun. Do the same for the AA Gun on the wall—watch for soldiers patrolling beyond the wall.

Move the Sapper and the Spy to the large yellow tanks near the entrance to the base. Plant a Timed Bomb next to the tanks. Leave the compound quickly and head around the edge of the base (past the Mines) toward the front of the submarine pen. Detonate the other Remote-Controlled Bombs. Scroll across the map to view your handiwork.

One AA Gun remains. Send the Spy to the watchtower beside the other beach. Use the Syringe to disable the guard looking out over the sea and tie him up. Move to the guard a level below the one you just dealt with and restrict his view of the water. Swim your squad from the submarine pen around the tower to the other beach.

Use the Sapper to cut the wire fence and check for Mines beyond it—there is a row across the beach. Crawl diagonally up the beach using the rocks for cover. Don't approach the wire yet—there are more Mines in front of it.

Use the Spy to distract or kill any guards that spot your approach to the far beach.

To give yourself time to find and defuse the Mines, send the Spy to distract the soldier patrolling the fence. When he's done so, send the Sapper through to knock out and tie up the distracted guard.

Now send the Spy to the bunker ahead and distract the guard there—don't let him look toward the beach. Crawl through the trees and knock out the Officer standing by the car. When the Spy gets in the car with the Security Papers (allowing him to drive into the base), the mini-objective is completed.

Climb the wall using the Diver's Grappling Hook or send the Thief up to drop down a Ladder.

To destroy the last AA Gun, return to the beach. The Spy must distract the guard on the watchtower located opposite building A-2. Doing so allows the Sapper to defuse the Mines close to the wall of the base. Use the Diver's Grappling Hook (or the Thief and the Ladder) to climb the wall, allowing the Sapper to plant the final charge next to the gun.

With a Timed Bomb, you have 20 seconds to run away. When the gun explodes, soldiers come to investigate—so don't hang around. Swim to the submarine pen, jump in the sub, and escape.

> **NOTE**
> You must have the Green Beret in your team to finish the mission. So if you haven't called him in, do so.

You can find one bonus photo piece in the barracks (**6**) opposite the Thief's original starting point. Two more can be found in the General's office (**7**, **8**), while another is located in a locker in the shower block (**9**). Slightly trickier, another bonus photo piece can be found in the subterranean bunker (**10**) near the large AA gun. The last bonus photo piece can be found in the small office (**11**) near the rear entrance of the base.

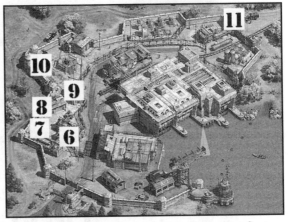

Still looking for those extra bonus photo pieces? You can find them all here.

You have three minutes to guide the motorboat around the twisting watercourse. You'll need patience rather than quick reflexes.

MISSION SECRET

Bonus photo pieces required: 11

This bonus mission simply involves guiding your Commando's motorboat around a water-based racecourse. The course itself has been marked off using mines—if you hit one your boat will explode. As the mission objectives point out, hitting any of the buoys that litter the course will slow you down. You need to complete the course in less than three minutes to successfully complete this bonus mission. It shouldn't pose a problem.

CHAPTER 8
WHITE DEATH

PRIMARY OBJECTIVES
- Contact the Sapper
- Rescue the Spy, the Thief, and the Allied sailors
- Recover the three parts of the Enigma machine
- Destroy the ship's engine room
- Rescue the ship's Captain
- The Green Beret and the Spy must use the plane to take the Enigma machine to HQ
- Escape in the submarine

SECONDARY OBJECTIVES
- Disable the ship's bow gun
- Disable the ship's central gun
- Disable the ship's stern gun
- Use the Balloon to obtain the explosives

WALKTHROUGH

In this mission, you start with only the Diver. Although the Green Beret, Thief, Spy, and Sapper are also featured in White Death, they're all being held captive in different parts of the map. So, you have to juggle the demands of the mission with freeing the other members of your team. But what looks like an impossible task at the outset can be broken down into a series of achievable phases. The first is to escape the submarine....

Rotate the screen around and take control of the Diver. Kill or knock out the guard outside your hiding place and take his weaponry. Search the nearby locker for a Pistol, Food, and some Snow Gear. The Snow Gear will automatically be worn by the Diver once it's placed in his inventory. There's also a **bonus** picture piece here. Look through the only door to spy on the guards beyond. When both have their backs to you, open the door, knock out the first and knife the second. Search the bodies. Search the lockers for First Aid Kits, the Green Beret's Decoy, the Grapple, Diving Gear, the Harpoon, and some Cigarettes (always useful). There's also a **bonus** picture piece here.

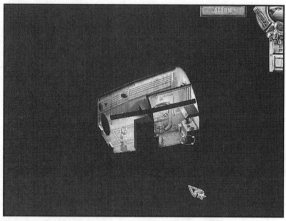

Rotate the view and take control of the Diver. Until you can free your fellow Commandos, this is a one-man mission.

From here you can go up (out of the sub) or into the next room that has two enemies in it. Take them out in the same way as before—move in, punch them both in quick succession ([Q]), and then kill one while you tie up the other. Perfect. Exits here include another door and a ladder up. Concentrate on clearing the lower level of the sub first. The next room is a long one—three compartments and three guards. Study their movements using [W] to look through the door. Wait until the roving guard has walked away from the soldier working nearest the door. Move in, kill him, and retrieve the Knife. Kill the next guard, and knock out the final one. Swift and efficient.

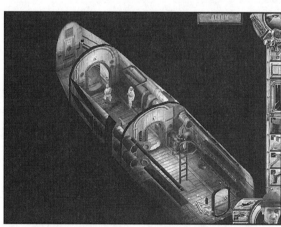

Your first task is to clear the submarine of enemy soldiers. Use the Diver's throwing Knife to silently rack up the body count.

Return to the room that has the map on the table. Use W on the ladder to see the guard on the level above. As soon as he starts to walk away from you, climb up and knock him out. Take his Machinegun. The ladder here leads up to the conning tower—two more enemies here. Don't be subtle. They won't see you coming up the ladder, so stand behind them and let rip with the Machinegun. Search the wooden box to get Grenades and a bottle of Poison. Go back to the room with the lockers in it. Use W again on the ladder to take a look outside.

Use W to look up the ladder and get a view of the submarine's deck area.

Zoom out the view and hit F11 so you can see where the enemies are. Guards are stationed at each end of the sub, while others patrol the mid-section.

Wait until the guard in white has his back to you and the guard wearing brown fatigues walks back down the gangplank. Quickly climb out on deck, staying low. Knife the guard in white, retrieve your Knife, and hide just behind the conning tower. Knife the guard in brown as he comes back and spots the dead guard. You'll need to be a good shot to get him before he runs out of range. Search both bodies for more ammo and then hide them on the deck behind the conning tower to ensure that they won't be spotted from the shore.

The only way off the sub is via the gangplank. Place a view marker (Tab) at the bottom of the gangplank so you can see which guards regularly look at it. When the guards aren't looking, run down the gangplank and hide at the side of the hut (A). Visibility is poor in these snowy conditions, so you won't be spotted.

Once you've cleared the sub's deck, you need to move quickly and stealthily down the gangplank to point A.

There are two Germans here, plus another who walks between the ship and the hut. Use the Cigarettes you found earlier to lure one of the Germans (an Officer) away from his position near the hut. Knock him out, tie him up, and search him. Take the keys. Knock out the remaining soldier, and hide both bodies. Use the Cigarettes again to lure in the wandering Lieutenant. Use the keys to open the door to the hut.

When the patrolling guard is standing next to the stairs, knife the stationary Lieutenant, and then walk

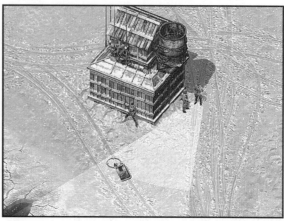

Most enemy soldiers are suckers for a free pack of Cigarettes. No wonder they lost the war…

around to knock out the guard. Walk up the stairs and look up the ladder. Climb up, knock out the guard, and free the Green Beret. Open the box to retrieve some more Snow Gear, plus the Green Beret's possessions—Knife, First Aid kit, Decoy Controller, and a Pistol. Search the guard to get a Machinegun.

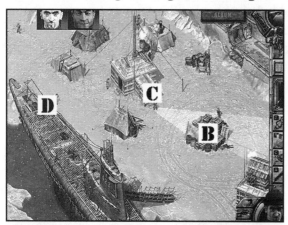

Although the area outside the sub is heavily guarded, just kill the guards one by one. Quietly does it.

Head back outside. Use the Green Beret to move all the dead bodies into the hut so they don't attract any attention. Leave the Green Beret in the hut and crawl the Diver behind the pile of crates and supplies (**B**). Zoom out and note the guard looking over the supplies (**C**) and the guard who patrols near the front of the sub (**D**). Lure guard **C** away from his post with Cigarettes, when the patrolling guard (**D**) is walking away from you—you don't want to attract them both. Kill guard **C** and carry the body back to the hut. If you didn't get a chance to pick up the Cigarettes as well, another guard will spot them. Let him have them. Watch him through the door of the hut until he returns to his regular route.

Return to the position behind the supply crates (**B**). Lure the guard patrolling along the sub away with more Cigarettes. Kill him and hide the body in the hut. Next, crawl along to a position between the sub and the small tent (**C**). Lure away the guard (**D**) standing outside the radio room with Cigarettes. Knife him and take his Machinegun. Carry his body back to the hut. You can now approach the radio building.

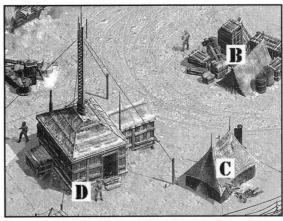

Use the cover provided by the supply crates and the tents to hide you from the patrolling German guards.

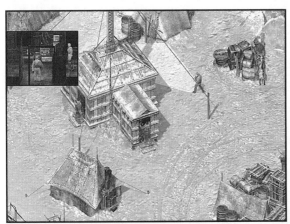

Look before you leap. Use W to peer through the door of the radio room to note the positions of the guards inside.

Look through the window into the radio building (from the small entrance). There are two guards in here—one patrolling, the other standing by the radio. Enter when the patrolling guard has his back to you and knife him. Then knife the second guard. Search the bodies for ammunition and weapons. Search the cupboard near the door you entered through to find another First Aid Kit and the third piece of the bonus picture. Finally, use the radio.

Before you free the Sapper in the small tent (**E**), take care of the remaining guards in this area. Use Cigarettes to lure them away from their positions and then knife them. When you deal with the two guards stationed outside tent **F**, make sure that you throw the Cigarettes behind tent **E**. This ensures that they don't distract other guards near the front of the submarine. Make sure you also knife the lured and distracted guard behind the tent for the same reason.

When there are no immediate threats, search tent **F** closest to the ship. The

The Sapper can be found in tent E. But you'll need to get the Snow Gear from tent F before he can leave his canvas prison.

wooden box inside contains extra Snow Gear, some Grenades, and a First Aid Kit. Take the Snow Gear to the Sapper—without it he'll freeze to death in these sub-zero conditions. Free the Sapper by clicking on him and holding [Shift]. Give the Grenades you've collected to the Sapper.

Here, guard, come get the nice Cigarettes! These guys will do anything for a free smoke.

Now you need to secure the Balloon. Doing so gives you almost complete control of this side of the ice. Stay low as you move toward it—you don't want the Machinegunner on the ship opening fire on you and wrecking all your good work so far. Lure the patrolling guards away from the Balloon with a trail of Cigarettes. You need at least two packs. Use [Tab] to monitor an enemy's vision so you know where to place them. Here, Cigarettes placed at points **1** and **2** attract the guard to the Commando's hiding place at **3**. You may have to use three packs to lure the last guard. Once the patrolling guards are dead, deal with the two guards next to the Balloon.

Climb on the ship by using the Diver's Grapple. Kill the Sniper standing at the stern. Next use the control panel opposite the raised gangplank and lower it. Move the rest of your team onboard. Forget about the starboard side of the ship for now. Instead, crawl your team along the deck, underneath the gunner until you reach a door. Look inside ([W]) before you charge in.

Watch what the guards do inside before making your move. Attack from behind and the side—kill the armed soldier first with a Knife, and knock out the soldier who attacks with his fists. Consider giving the Diver two Knives so he can kill multiple guards quickly and quietly.

Use the Diver's Grapple to climb onto the ship. Activate the control panel nearby to lower the wooden gangplank.

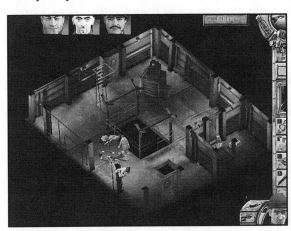

The Diver's ability to throw his Knife is immensely useful in this mission. Consider giving him the Green Beret's blade, too.

Look into the next room, then move in when the guard turns his back on you. There are some guards in a small room here. Open the door, stand back, and throw a Knife at the guard you can see. When the other one examines his comrade's body, kill him, too. You can't use firearms here—the alarm will go off immediately and most of the ship's guards will run into the room to investigate. Save your bullets for now. Search the wooden box here to find a Remote-Controlled Bomb, a Timed Bomb, Grenades, and some Poison. There's one other door out of this room and ladders leading up and down.

The next room is a long corridor connected to eight rooms. Look through the door and enter the room when the guard is standing close to the door with his back to you. Knock him out and tie him up. Throw a Knife at the next guard (**A**), taking care not to alert the guard sitting in **B**—the door to this room is open. Monitor the vision of **B** and lure him out of the room with Cigarettes. Kill him with the Diver's second Knife.

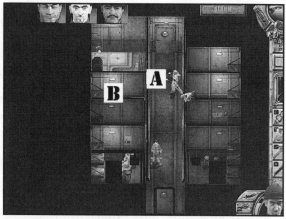

Search the rooms that DON'T have guards in them. You can come back and examine the guarded doors later with the Spy.

Search the empty rooms to find another set of Snow Gear, more Timed Bombs, Grenades, and other items. Finally, free the Captain—he's in a cell opposite the shower.

Look through the next door and enter the storeroom beyond when the guard walks away from you. Dispose of him and then search the four lockers to find more supplies. There's also another piece of the **bonus** picture here. Now retrace your steps back to the large room with the ladders (see earlier figure). It's easier to head upward for now. As usual, watch the routes of the guards in the room above before going into it. It's difficult to get your bearings—move the view until you can see the soldier and the technician. Enter the room when the soldier is walking toward the technician. Make sure that the Diver has two Knives so he can dispatch the two soldiers quickly.

This room has four possible exits. Two lead out to the deck and two lead farther into the ship. Look through the door (**C**) closest to the ladder you just climbed—press **F10** to illuminate the doors, it's dark here. Two guards should be endlessly circling the machinery of

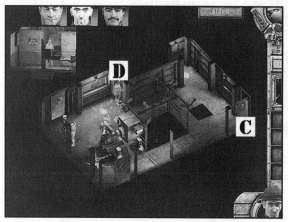

The exit (**C**) leads to the first gun mechanism. Plant a Timed Bomb here to disable the gun above.

one of the deck guns. Wait until they walk past you, then knock them out in quick succession. Kill one to prevent him from waking up before you've tied up the other one. The alarm may go off at this point, but you should be safe enough. Plant a Timed Bomb here to disable the cannon above. You have 20 seconds to run like hell.

Go to the only other door that doesn't lead you outside (**D**). Give the Diver the Green Beret's Knife if you haven't already done so. Enter when the patrolling guard is talking to the technician in the small side room. Walk in, throw the first Knife at the technician working in the large room, then move quickly to throw the second Knife at the guard. Finally, rush up and knock out the remaining technician. Tie him up and retrieve your weapons.

There's a cupboard on the wall here. Open it to find another piece of the **bonus** picture, a First Aid Kit, and more Snow Gear. There are two exits from this area—one leads outside, the other up to the bridge.

To clear the bridge, look through the door and wait until the patrolling guard has descended the steps to stand in the corridor below. Open the door and throw a Knife at the soldier. This leaves only the bridge staff. As one Officer looks out the windows, throw a Knife at the nearest man and then throw the second Knife at the window-gazing Officer. The last man has his back to you, so knock him out and tidy up. Search the desk to find the Enigma codes, Enigma cylinders, and the Enigma machine itself. The doors and the ladder lead outside. Retrace your steps back to the room with the ladders (see earlier figure).

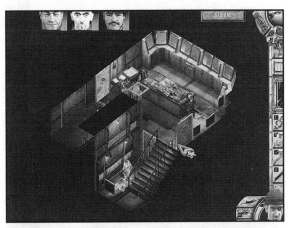

The Enigma machine can be found in the desk on the ship's bridge. Kill the Officers and take it back.

This time, look down the ladder. Your view is limited, and you can't see anything. But there are a lot of enemy soldiers down there. Trust me. You probably won't even make it off the ladder. There's a safer way to reach the room below.

Head out onto the deck. Crawl the length of the ship to the stern. Guide the Captain back to the sub for safe-keeping—if he dies, the mission is a failure. Entice the patrolling soldier (E) on the starboard side using Cigarettes, and throw a Knife when he gets close enough. Next, crawl around to the small ladder and enter the door (F) between the two guns. In this small room, a ladder leads up to the roof, while another leads down into the bowels of the ship. You need to go down.

To disable the rear guns, head back outside and enter the ship through door F.

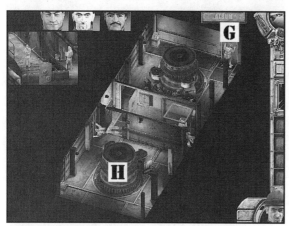

The two gun mechanisms here also need to be destroyed on your way to completing your primary mission objectives.

Bring up the Sapper and throw a Grenade down the ladder. Watch as the guards below come to investigate and then throw down a second one to kill them. Wait until the alarm has finished blaring, and go down the ladder. Kill any guards that remain. Note the location of the door that leads into the engine room (G). Move your men into the room with the gun mechanism that is farthest from this door (H).

Line up the Green Beret with a full Machinegun on Standing Coverage ([X]), so he can aim through the door into the other rooms. If you have another full Machinegun, give it to the Diver and set him to auto-fire through the doorway. Get the Sapper to plant a Timed Bomb next to the gun mechanism ([I]) near the door to the engine room ([G]). Move him to stand behind the prone, auto-firing Green Beret. When the charge goes off, it'll attract the attention of the troops in the engine room. Wait for them to arrive and then kill them with Grenades and Machinegun fire.

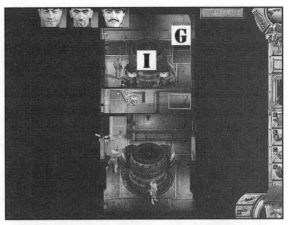

Use the Machineguns that you've been picking up to set up a trap for the enemies in the engine room through door [G].

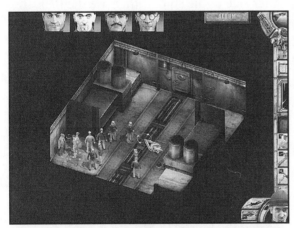

Free the captured sub crew, the Spy, and the Thief. The Spy is vital to completing the rest of the mission.

Plant a Timed Bomb next to the remaining gun mechanism and head into the engine room. It should be empty. Look through the door on the opposite side of the room. There may be some guards in here who weren't lured out by your explosion. Kill the first in the corridor and then lure out the others. Place the dead body in front of the door and knock on the wall ([Q]) to get their attention. When they come out to investigate, kill them. Examine the box here to get the Thief's Lockpick and the Spy's Syringe. The keys you stole earlier open the locked door at the end of this room where you'll find the sub crew, the Thief, and the Spy.

Release the Thief, the Spy, and the sub crew. Guide the sub crew and the Captain back to the submarine. Give the Thief the extra Snow Gear, and borrow a German uniform for the Spy. Any rank will do for now. Finally, place a Timed Bomb in the engine room and run away to avoid the inevitable blast.

Plant a Timed Bomb next to the machinery in the engine room. Bang goes another mission objective!

It's easier to fight your way AROUND the ship than to fly OVER it in the Balloon.

Now you need to get to the plane on the other side of the ship. Either use the Balloon to fly there or fight your way around the ice to get to the plane. To be honest, it's easier on foot. Dress the Spy in an Officer's uniform—there should be one in the hut where you stored all the bodies earlier. Use the Spy,

dressed as a German, to distract the guards en route to the plane. Use the Diver to kill them with his Knife. Start by killing the guard near the bow of the sub.

Two more guards patrol the area in front of the ship. Kill these using the Diver and the Spy. Note the guard standing on the bow of the ship. You can kill him by crossing the small gap in the ice and climbing the anchor chain. Work your way to the plane, distracting the

Use the Spy and the Diver in combination to distract and disable the guards who stand between you and the plane.

soldiers or luring them out of position with Cigarettes. Remember, the Spy can disable guards with his Syringe—two doses to knock them out temporarily, three to kill...

When you've cleared the path to the plane, clear the patrolling soldiers around the snow mound (**A**) behind it. Use the Spy to distract the guards on the raised section at **B**. Turn your attention to the guards on the hill— again the Spy and the Diver make a great attacking team. Free Cigarettes are your ticket to success. The crates (**C**) on the raised section (**B**) contain extra Remote-Controlled Bombs, Grenades, and Timed Bombs. Not that you'll need them now.

To complete the mission, move the Green Beret and the Spy into the aircraft. One character needs to be holding the Enigma machine and its related parts. Note that the Spy can't enter the plane while he's disguised. Also, the rest of your team need to be moved into the submarine so that they can escape. If you want to complete the **bonus** picture, the last photo fragment is located in the part of the ship where you found the Captain (see the figure showing the room without guards). Use the Spy (dressed as an Officer) to search the rooms with enemy guards inside.

MISSION SECRET

Bonus photo pieces required: 6

If you were expecting the bonus missions to be simple, this one will come as something of a surprise. The overall objective (escape the map in an enemy vehicle) is complicated by the fact that you need to kill an enemy sniper, murder a group of Grenadiers, and steal an

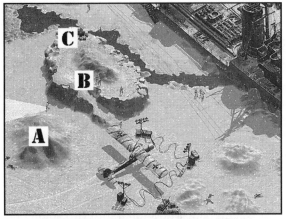

You must kill the guards patrolling **A** and **B** so that you can get into the plane unseen.

The Spy won't be able to get into the plane until you remove his disguise. But don't leave him outside too long...

amphibious tank on the way. Your Commandos—Green Beret, Sniper, Driver, Diver, and Sapper—start behind a pile of logs and face several immediate threats.

Start by luring the wandering, white-shirted soldier to the logs using the Sniper's Cigarettes—throw them well *behind* the logs so nobody else can see them. Knock out the soldier and tie him up. Next, throw the Cigarettes to the other side of the log pile to attract the Lieutenant who's talking to two soldiers in the center of this first area. Concentrate on killing the armed guards first. Use the

Use the skills you've learned so far to lure away the soldiers that are facing your start position.

Sniper to take out the two soldiers who were chatting to the Lieutenant, then shoot the soldier sitting on the logs when he runs to investigate. Use the Green Beret to stab the rest of the unarmed soldiers. Open the wooden box to get Gas Grenades and Molotov Cocktails. Before you get into the amphibious tank, use the Sniper to shoot the soldier on the far bank.

Although the amphibious tank is armored, the Grenadiers can still blow it up while your Commandos are inside.

Swim the Sniper ashore and shoot the other sniper hiding next to the log pile (you may have to stand up quickly to get a shot in). Crawl the Green Beret ashore and aim at the two soldiers talking in front of the log pile. Use X to specify autofire and let him shoot the two men, plus two more who run to investigate. Search the bodies for ammunition and the wooden box nearby for Grenades, a Remote-Controlled Bomb, and a Flamethrower. Throw a Grenade to kill all of the Grenadiers. Move the Sapper to search the wooden box near the dead Grenadiers, then throw more Grenades to kill the remaining soldiers. Mission complete!

CHAPTER 9
TARGET: BURMA

PRIMARY OBJECTIVES

- Rescue the spiritual leader
- Eliminate the tyrant
- Rescue the Gurkhas
- Order the Gurkhas to operate the radio
- Escape on the barge with the spiritual leader

SECONDARY OBJECTIVES

- Contact the fat man and arm the Gurkhas

WALKTHROUGH

In this mission, you must infiltrate a heavily garrisoned Japanese stronghold. The spiritual leader is located in a large house on the central island, while the Gurkhas are being held in tunnels under the stronghold. The Sniper plays a vital role if you can find more ammunition.

To get across the river and inside the stronghold, you need to secure the side of the river you start the mission on. Start by taking out the guards in your vicinity. Zoom out so you know where the guards are in relation to your Commandos.

Take control of the Green Beret and kill the guard second from the bridge (A). Stab him when the guard standing nearest the bridge (B) isn't looking, then drag the body behind the trees. Return to stab the guard nearest the bridge (A). Search both bodies for weapons.

Monitor the vision of guard B so you can sneak up behind guard A and kill him. Hide the body, then kill guard B.

Zoom out to note the positions of the guards on this side of the river. You need to reach the bridge at the top of this screen.

Monitor the vision of the guard patrolling the waterfront (C). Hide behind one of the low walls and creep up behind him as he looks out over the water. Kill him with the Knife and hide the body. Next, move up behind the guard who has his back to you (D). Stab him when the patrolling guard ahead (B) isn't looking. Again, carry the body out of sight. This leaves the patrolling guard (E). The Green Beret can deal with him, too. Wait until he stands closest to your position, then move up behind him as he turns to continue his route. It's a long walk, but the Green Beret will easily make it. Nobody will spot you or hear you dispatch the guard. Hide the body before you move on.

Still controlling the Green Beret, approach the small bridge that leads to the central island. Crawl up behind one of the statues, staying out of sight of the patrolling Officer here. Follow the Officer as he walks away from the bridge to have a cigarette in the trees, and stab him. Search him for a pack of Cigarettes—vital Commando equipment.

Use the statues near the bridge to hide from the patrolling Officer. Kill him when he walks away from the bridge.

Shoot the guard on the balcony at **F**. Doing so will allow you to swim across the river without being spotted.

Bring up the Sniper and use one of his five bullets to take out the guard who patrols the first floor balcony of the building near the bridge (**F**). Make sure that you shoot him when he's out of the sight of the guards below. With this guard out of the way, the Green Beret can double back, swim across the river, and crawl up the steps at **G**. Monitor the vision of the guard standing at the bottom of the steps nearby (**I**). Stab the guard (**H**) without being spotted, then carry his body out of sight.

Lure guard **I** out of position using the Cigarettes you picked up earlier. With all immediate threats taken care of, bring the rest of your team across the river. Use the Thief to climb onto the balcony of the building where you shot guard **F**. Drop the Thief's Ladder over the side so that the other Commandos can climb up. Move the Green Beret around to the doorway on the balcony and look through it (**W**). The room beyond leads to a tunnel that comes out into the river below. This secret entrance can be found underwater between the two sets of steps. Since you've made it this far, you can ignore it.

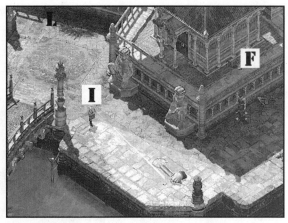

The old Cigarette trick rarely fails. Use the Green Beret to stab guard **I** as he passes by your hiding place.

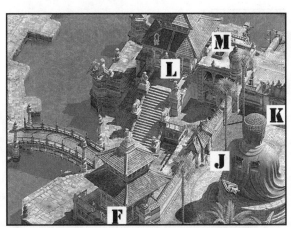

The spiritual leader is unguarded in building **L**. Freeing him, however, isn't the hard part. Escaping is.

Move the Green Beret past the small archway here—notice the guard (**J**) on the other side who's eyeing a courtyard that contains a giant statue. Place the Decoy to one side of the arch and stand on the other side. Set off the Decoy and stab guard **J** as he investigates the noise. You can repeat this process for a second guard (**K**) standing in the courtyard. To draw him into the range of the Decoy, you'll need to use a pack of Cigarettes as an extra lure. Hide the bodies on the balcony at **F**.

Send one of your Commandos up the large steps (**L**) to free the spiritual leader. Freeing him isn't the hard part. Escaping with him on the barge (located on the opposite side of the map) is another matter. Move the spiritual leader to a safe position with the rest of the squad. For now, the balcony at **F** is perfect. Once the spiritual leader

is safe, send the Green Beret up the ladder next to the large stairway. Enter the building through the hole on the roof (M).

Stab the guard inside the building. Ignore the two Japanese soldiers in the ante-room. Instead, climb down the ladder in the center of the room to the tunnels below. Here you'll find the captured Gurkhas—walk close to each one and you'll subsequently be able to select them like any other character. The only other exit here is via an under-water tunnel. It's easier to retrace your steps, climbing up the ladder and out onto the roof. Once outside, move the Gurkhas to a safe hiding place. You'll need them to operate the radio when you find it.

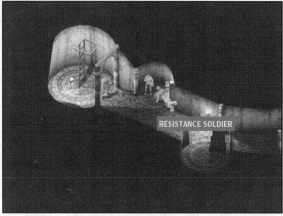

You'll find the Gurkhas in a tunnel under the building where you found the spiritual leader.

NOTE

As you progress through this level, make sure you pick up as many Rifles as you can. You'll eventually need to arm the Gurkhas.

Enemy snipers are covering the court-yard and the entrance to the giant statue. You'll never make it to the other side, so a different approach is needed. Move your team down the Ladder, picking up the Ladder as you leave, and work your way along the wall toward the barge. You can't reach the barge directly from here because the bridge support blocks the path. Use the Thief to climb the wall so he arrives in the courtyard just behind another guard. Drop the Ladder again to allow the Green Beret and Sniper to follow. Use the Green Beret to stab the guard (A).

Move your team along the wall. Use the Thief to climb up the wall and to drop the Ladder for the others.

Make sure the Thief retrieves the Ladder. There's nothing of interest in the building that guard **A** was protecting, so crawl along to the next available door (**B**), keeping tight to the wall. Press F10 to highlight it if you can't see it right away. This building is home to four snipers—two on the balcony at **C** and two more on the roof of the building (**D**). Killing them and taking their ammunition greatly increases your chances of completing the mission. The Sniper can kill enemy soldiers with one shot. His gun is practically silent and has a long firing range.

Deal with the enemy snipers in this building and you can move freely across the courtyard.

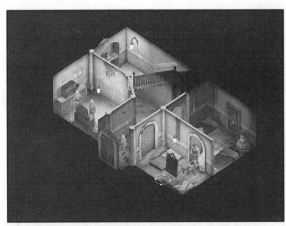

Move through the building methodically, patiently waiting for the right moment to attack the patrolling soldiers.

Enter the ground level of the snipers' building and quickly stab the nearby guard. There's a second guard patrolling the corridor and several Officers in a small room. Press F10 to illuminate the two cupboards in this small room—there's a **bonus** picture piece in there if you can reach it. Leave it for now or use one of the Driver's Molotovs to take out several of the Officers at once. There's one moment when all three stand close together. The cupboards contain Smoke Grenades, more Molotovs, a First Aid Kit, a Gas Grenade, Binoculars, and another Trip Wire.

Head up the stairway. Stab the guard looking through the window, then take out the lone soldiers in two of the four rooms. The two soldiers in the last room can be dispatched with a Molotov, but there's not much else of interest here. Keep moving and climb the ladder to the third floor. This level is packed with Japanese soldiers, so ignore it and climb the ladder again to the fourth level. Quickly stab the two snipers here before they can get off a shot, then steal their Rifles. You can give these to your own Sniper when you leave.

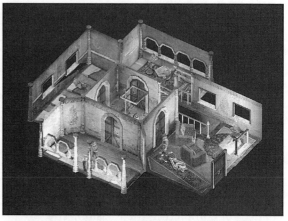

Two snipers are on the fourth floor of this building. Quickly move the Green Beret up the ladders and stab them.

Use your Sniper to shoot the two guards stationed at either side of the large green-roofed archway.

Return to the second floor to the room with two brown armchairs. Look through the doorway to see the two snipers on the balcony outside. Before you can safely dispose of them, you need to shoot the two guards standing at the gate directly opposite this building. Switch characters and bring the Sniper in to join the Green Beret. Use W to look out the window onto the balcony and the gate beyond. Shoot the two soldiers at the gate. Before you attack the snipers, use the Driver to set a Trap on the staircase in this room. A lone soldier will come to investigate when you kill the first sniper. Placing the Trap ensures that he is killed before he can attack any of your troops. Kill both snipers and take their ammunition.

Move the Sniper so he can look out over the smaller courtyard. In addition to the guard (⒠) in the courtyard below, there's another sniper in the red-roofed building opposite (⒡). Use your Sniper to take out the enemy sharpshooter. Send the Green Beret through the double doors to emerge behind the guard (⒠). Kill him and carry the body inside. Zoom out and highlight any nearby soldiers by pressing ⒡⒒. There's a guard who wanders back and forth between the barge on the river and this courtyard.

When the coast is clear, move the Green Beret across the small courtyard

There's another sniper hiding on the top floor of building ⒡. You need to get rid of him before you can cross this courtyard.

to enter building ⒡, where you just shot the sniper. Climb down the ladder and kill the guard on the lower level. Then climb to the top of the building to retrieve the dead sniper's ammunition. There are two wooden boxes here, but you can't open them yet. Remember, you need to collect extra weapons to arm the Gurkhas. Pick up any Rifles that you come across. They'll be vital later in the mission.

The strategy here is to work your way around the edge of the map, killing guards as you go.

Move the Green Beret to the ground floor of building ⒡. Look through the wooden doors to watch the patrolling guard. When he's close enough, open the door and stab him. Hide his body in building ⒡. Move along the waterfront and kill the next guard.

Next, approach the window of the nearby building ⒢. Send the Thief inside via the window, using him to drop the Ladder so the Green Beret can follow.

Once inside, lure the first of the two guards away from his position using Cigarettes. Sneak up and stab the second. Search the two items of furniture on this level to find Gas Grenades, Molotovs, Smoke Grenades, and another **bonus** picture piece. Move upstairs and eliminate the guard.

Leave building G through the front door. Drop down behind the guard closest to the building and stab him. Cross the street and kill the other guard talking to the monks.

Leave the building and kill the guards standing in the street—one stands in front of the building, the other stands in the garden opposite.

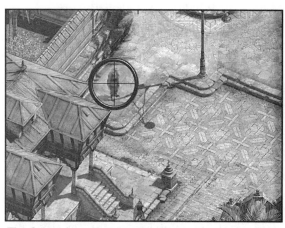

The Sniper is perfect for taking out enemy soldiers at distance. Best of all, the Sniper Rifle is almost completely silent.

Bring up the Sniper to take care of the next two guards from distance. Monitor the vision of the farthest one and shoot the closest guard when he's not being observed. Quickly take down the second. The dead bodies may attract one or two additional guards, so keep the Sniper in position and listen for the warning shouts. Shoot any investigating guards once they're in range.

Move on to the next building. Send the Green Beret through the topmost of the three doors (**H**). Kill the Japanese soldier inside, then climb down the ladder. Lure the next guard away from his room using Cigarettes. The two remaining guards are easily dispatched with a Molotov from the Driver. Search the three items of furniture here for a Shovel, a Trip Wire, and a **bonus** picture piece. Look up the ladder in this room and time your ascent to the room above.

Kill the two guards, then search the locker to find Sleeping Pills, a First Aid Kit, and another **bonus** picture piece. Climb back down and exit via the doorway that leads out next to the green-roofed archway.

Use the Green Beret to clear out the buildings, knifing any enemy soldiers that you find. Gunfire will only set off the alarm.

There are too many guards outside building (**I**). Luckily there's a back entrance in the large courtyard opposite the statue.

Continuing to work your way around the edge of this map, you now need to enter the next building (**I**). Entering via the riverside is too dangerous, but there's a way in via the large courtyard. Choose the far entrance first—an open archway (**J**). The Green Beret should have no problem moving from room to room stabbing the soldiers here. Search the furniture to find more Sleeping Pills, two **bonus** picture pieces, and more Gas and Smoke Grenades.

Locate the window next to the green gate. Use the Sniper to aim through the window and shoot the guard patrolling the back room. When he's dead, send the Thief through the window and drop the Ladder to let the Green Beret and the Driver up. Take out the three soldiers with a Molotov. Find and kill the Officer lying in bed. There are two passages leading down and a stairway leading up. There's nothing of interest on the lower level, so take the stairway.

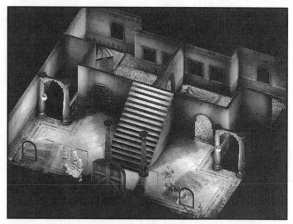

Shoot the guard through the window, then climb inside. Use a Molotov to kill the three Japanese soldiers here.

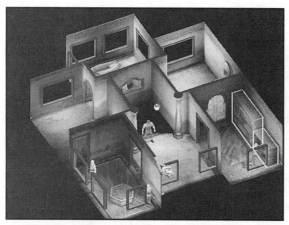

Use F10 to highlight important items of furniture. The two cupboards here are outlined in green.

Kill the guard next to the large cupboards and search them for a **bonus** picture piece, a Ladder, extra Grenades, and Molotovs. Bring the Sniper up to this floor and use the high vantage point to shoot at the guards across the river. Take out as many as you can.

Send the Green Beret through the gate to take out the patrolling guard. Move the rest of your Commandos to the corner of the building with the green turreted roof. Use the Sniper to shoot one of the guards through the window. Distract the guard standing in front of the building with some Cigarettes and draw him into the Sniper's gun sight. A second guard should spot the dead body and run to investigate—shoot him, too.

If you can't sneak into a building unnoticed, use the Sniper to shoot THROUGH the window from the outside.

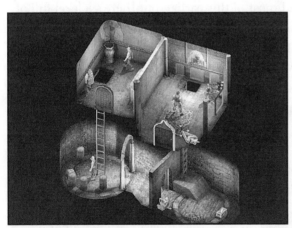

Talk to the fat man to complete one of the secondary objectives, and get one step closer to finishing the mission.

Enter the building. Descend the ladder when the soldier below walks into the adjacent room. Stab him when he returns. Climb up the second ladder and stab the soldier in the room directly above. Talk to the fat man there. After you've done this, you can access the wooden crates (plus those you found earlier). Next, shoot the remaining guard on this side of the river.

Bring around the Gurkhas and the spiritual leader. You only need to equip a single Gurkha with a spare Rifle to complete the objective. Press W and click on a Gurkha to open his inventory. Ultimately, you need to equip four of the five Gurkhas with weapons.

Move the Green Beret and an unarmed Gurkha to the radio room (**A**). Kill the guards inside on the first floor, then search the cupboard for a **bonus** picture piece. Climb up the ladder and kill the soldiers in the radio room above. Before you activate the radio (which calls in Japanese reinforcements), double back and clear out some of the buildings. Doing so also allows you to pick up extra ammunition for the Gurkhas (who will fight the last battle) and to search for any **bonus** picture pieces that you haven't found yet.

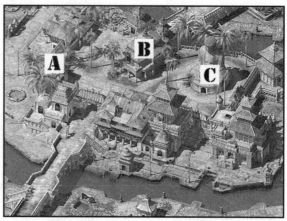

Note the location of the radio room. Only one of the Gurkhas can operate the equipment there.

Form a three-man team—Green Beret, Sniper, and Driver. Start with the large building next to the bridge (**B**). You cleared most of this earlier, but there's a level full of guards upstairs. Move onto the next house, clearing it of enemy soldiers as you go. The final pieces of the **bonus** picture can be found on the ground floor of the same building where you found the spiritual leader—enter via the double doors around the back. Finally, move onto the statue (**C**).

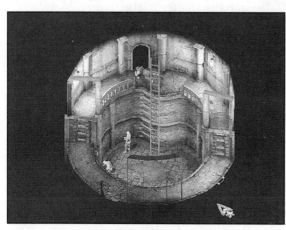

Clear out the statue in the courtyard so that the soldiers can't help out the reinforcements that eventually arrive.

Have the Green Beret crawl into the statue and, staying low, knife the guard nearby. Pan the view around until you can see the two guards working on the level below. Wait until the patrolling guard walks away from the ladder that leads down to the lower level. Climb down and stab the guard, then kill the one kneeling nearby. Climb the ladder again and walk around the inside of the statue to the door opposite the one you entered through. Knife the two soldiers working in the corridor. The two exits here lead out into the river.

Return to the main part of the statue. Climb the long ladder to the level above. Kill the guard here and climb up again, killing two more guards.

Now would be an ideal time to Quicksave. Before you use the radio, equip four Gurkhas with Rifles and with as many rounds of ammunition as you can find. Place all four Gurkhas across the road so they have an arc of fire across the main bridge out of the stronghold. Set them to provide Ground Coverage. Bring up the Sniper and be ready to use him to add extra long-range fire to that of the Gurkhas. As soon as

Place the Gurkhas in a line across the bridge so that they can all shoot down the length of the bridge. This is where the Japanese reinforcements will come from.

the fifth Gurkha activates the radio, a massive contingent of Japanese reinforcements will arrive. Rather than let them get into the stronghold, cut them off on the bridge. The Gurkhas should mow them down easily.

Once the reinforcements have been massacred, use the Sniper to assassinate the tyrant. Make your way to the barge.

When the battle is almost over, run up and steal the tyrant's car, driving it down the bridge. The tyrant will subsequently appear on foot. Take control of the Sniper and shoot him. To complete the mission, guide your Commandos and the spiritual leader to the barge. Once all of your men are in, the barge slowly (and automatically) cruises around the river and off the screen.

MISSION SECRET

Bonus photo pieces required: 9

In this bonus mission, organize a small band of ten Allied soldiers to resist an invasion by a superior German force. In addition to the ten troopers (each armed with a Rifle and unlimited ammunition), you control the Green Beret, Sniper, Sapper and the Driver. The key to success here is to find a defensible position with long fields of fire and to use your resources wisely.

The Sapper is armed with ten Mines and five Grenades. Use all of them.

Set up defensive positions so that you catch the enemy in a crossfire. Avoid placing your defenders too close together—the enemy has Grenadier units that can wipe out your forces in seconds if you don't spread them out. Place Allied soldiers in advanced positions and kill the enemy before they reach your start point. Use the Sapper to set all of the Mines. Finally, move the Sapper along the bottom of the screen and sneak him up to the wall in front of the enemy. Throw a Grenade into the ordered ranks of German soldiers to kill as many as possible. Then run like hell back to your own lines. It's a tough mission. It may take a long time before you master it.

CHAPTER 10

BRIDGE OVER THE RIVER KWAI

PRIMARY OBJECTIVES

- Rescue Guinness
- Obtain the explosives
- Find the bridge's weak spot by showing Guinness the model
- Plant the explosives
- Summon the train by sending a telegraph

SECONDARY OBJECTIVES

- Cross the river on an elephant
- Rescue the prisoners

WALKTHROUGH

The deeper into *Commandos 2* you play, the bigger and more challenging the missions become. Bridge Over the River Kwai is no exception. You start with four Commandos—Thief, Driver, Diver, and Green Beret. As usual, a stealthy approach is required to complete the mission objectives. Once the alarm is raised, there are scores of Japanese soldiers waiting to kill you. Of course, you might just get captured instead of killed (it *is* possible). But don't count on it.

Use the Green Beret to knife the two guards who patrol the fence next to your starting position. Hide the bodies next to the cliff face. You also need to get rid of the guard patrolling the front of the elephant pen. Fortunately, he can be lured away using a pack of Cigarettes. But be cautious: These Cigarettes may also attract the attention of the guards in the watchtower beyond the trees. Don't worry if you lose them. You can retrieve them when you eliminate the watchtower guards.

From your starting position, kill the three guards that patrol the edge of the elephant pen.

Use the Diver to eliminate the guards by the car and at the watchtower. Kill them one by one throwing the Knife.

The two guards in the watchtower rotate their watch. While one looks out over the river from the tower, the other climbs down the ladder to look at the car below. After a few moments, this guard returns to the watchtower and the other one climbs down to do the same thing. From your starting position, take control of the Diver and crawl up to the trees near the car. When one of the guards is climbing the ladder back to the watchtower, walk behind the Japanese soldier reading the paper and hide behind the corner of the wooden building. The next time the guard comes down, looks, and then turns to go, quickly throw a Knife at the paper-reading soldier. You'll have just enough time to pick up your Knife, grab the body, and head back to the start position before the guards turn around.

With one guard dead, return to the trees and then back to the corner of the building. When one of the guards comes down to look at the car, knife him like you did the previous one. Carry his body back to the start position. With no one to relieve him, the last guard will dutifully stay at his post. Simply climb up the ladder to the tower and stab him. Take control of the Thief and unlock the metal crate you find here. Take the Machinegun, Molotov Cocktails, and Smoke Grenades. Retrieve your Cigarettes from the dead guard if you lost them earlier.

Kill the final guard on the watchtower and use the Thief to unlock the metal crate you find there.

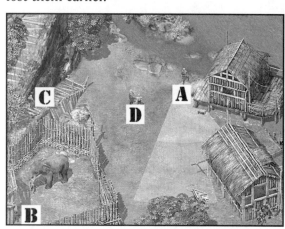

Secure your position on this side of the river by killing all of the guards. Zoom out so you can see them all.

Using the Diver, lure the patrolling guard (A) from his position near the far building. Kill him when he's close enough. Carry his body away so it doesn't raise the alarm. Now do the same for the guard stationed inside the elephant compound (B). Draw him out with the promise of free Cigarettes and then bury the Knife in his back. Walk to the edge of the elephant pen and throw a Knife at the guard standing on the slope (C). Killing him first ensures that he won't be attracted by the Cigarette trick you play on the two guards that remain (D). If you haven't already given the Diver the Green Beret's Knife, do it now.

Kill the two men talking in the middle of this area. Use Tab to monitor the vision of the guard facing the river. Move the Diver to the corner of the building near the two men. Lie on the floor and throw a pack of Cigarettes into the center of his vision. Staying low so he doesn't see you, throw a Knife at him. When you've retrieved your Knife, dispatch the other guard (who has his back to you). Use the Thief to unlock the metal crate here and take the First Aid Kit and pack of Cigarettes you find.

Lure troublesome guards away from their positions by using a pack of Cigarettes. No item is more useful in COMMANDOS 2.

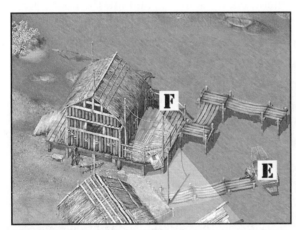

Eliminate all the guards OUTSIDE before you turn your attention to those INSIDE the buildings here.

Use F11 to identify the threats that remain—there's one soldier messing around with a boat (E) and another at the back of the second building (F). There's also a guard patrolling the river-bank that goes under the bridge. Lure guard F away from his position by throwing some Cigarettes directly onto the platform where he's standing. As he moves to get the Cigarettes, he'll spot the dead guard on the watchtower. This brings him out of the house altogether. Wait for him and dispatch him with the throwing Knife. His death allows you to kill the man next to the boat (E) and gives you unwatched access to the building next to the watchtower.

Return the Knife to the Green Beret. The building next to the watchtower is a boathouse. The soldiers in here don't move and are unarmed. Simply send in the Green Beret and stab the soldiers one by one. They can only respond with ineffectual punches that won't cause any lasting damage. When you emerge victorious, search the box on the table to find some Wirecutters, Cigarettes, and a piece of the **bonus** picture. Use the Thief to unlock the metal crate here. Take the Ladder that you find inside.

Now clean out the other building.

Look before you leap. Use W to peer inside buildings before you go charging in.

Using the Green Beret, look through the doorway—there's a single occupant you can see, and three you can't. As usual, pick your moment, enter the room, and kill the guard in the bedroom. A Japanese soldier regularly walks from the balcony (where there are two more soldiers) into the hallway. Knife him as he passes the doorway. Search the chest of drawers in the bedroom to find a pair of Binoculars, some more Molotov Cocktails,

It's easy to miss the guard who patrols the riverbank under the bridge. Kill him as he walks away from the buildings.

a Grapple, and a piece of the **bonus** picture. Leave the remaining guards— they're more trouble than they're worth.

Deal with the last guard hiding out near the side of the bridge. Wait near the slope until he starts to walk away from you, then use the Diver to simply run up behind him and knife him. Now follow the path under the bridge and clear the guards that remain on this side of the river.

Next you need to clear the guards patrolling the railroad track above. Give the Diver two Knives and guide him up the slope until you're almost at the top. Throw a pack of Cigarettes toward guard **A** to attract guards **B** and **C**. With two Knives, the Diver can quickly dispatch the guards from his hiding place. Retrieve both Knives and throw another pack of Cigarettes toward the nearest pole (**D**). This attracts the attention of guard **E**. As this guard gets closer, he'll be drawn toward the soldiers you have killed. Knife him when he gets close enough. The remaining soldiers here have their backs to you. Kill or knock out the one farthest from the bridge (**F**). Then lure the final guard (**G**) away from his position. This ensures that his death won't alert another soldier on the bridge itself.

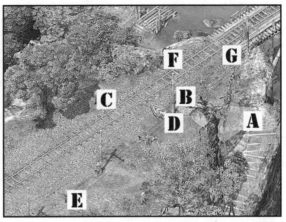

Take out the guards stationed at the end of the bridge so you can move onto it safely later in the mission.

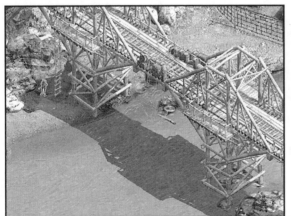

Swim across to the far bridge support, taking care to avoid the patrolling guard on the riverbank.

Once the end of the bridge has been cleared, go back down the slope and under the bridge using the path. Take control of the Diver. Look across the river at the far bridge support. Watch for the Japanese soldier patrolling back and forth between the ladder and the prison compound where Guinness is being kept.

As the guard walks away from the ladder on his patrol route, swim across the river and up to the bridge support, so you're hiding behind the nearest wooden strut. Throw a packet of Cigarettes near the ladder to entice the patrolling guard. Use the throwing Knife to kill him. Leave the body where it falls.

Once again, by using Cigarettes your Commandos can move enemy soldiers into positions where they can be killed easily.

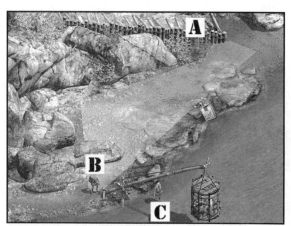

You need to kill guard **B** before you can attack **C** and free the caged prisoners.

Crawl to the log slope (**A**) and hide at the bottom, behind the low log wall. Monitor the vision of the patrolling soldier (**B**) who walks along the riverbank past the caged prisoners nearby. Use Cigarettes to lure him away from his route and kill him when he gets close enough to spot you. Next, wait for the soldier guarding the caged prisoners (**C**) to walk toward the river. Creep up and knife him before he starts to walk back.

Ignore the caged prisoners for now. Keep moving along the riverbank to where some Japanese soldiers are guarding prisoners and an elephant. Crawl toward them and hide behind the large rock. Knife the guard looking out over the river. His death brings one of the remaining guards to investigate, which should not be a problem if your Diver is carrying two Knives.

Finish off the last soldier and search the box for items. To free the caged prisoners, use a Knife on the end of the wooden pole. This causes the cage to drop into the water. Before doing this, equip your Diver with his Diving Gear (D). Once the cage falls, get into the water and dive under (B). You have 30 seconds to open the door of the cage. Note that you'll only be allowed to open it once the cage has hit the bottom of the river.

Hide behind the large rock in the center of the riverbank so the three Japanese soldiers here don't spot you.

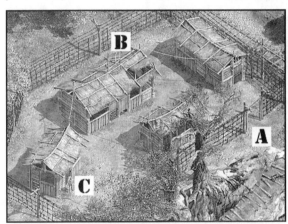

The prison compound here is lightly guarded. It's also where you'll find the explosives needed to blow up the bridge.

Move the rest of your team across the river and congregate at the bottom of the log slope. Send the Diver crawling up the slope. Note the guard at the top (**A**), lure him out of position with some Cigarettes, and kill him. Another guard should quickly come to investigate his comrade's death. Use the Diver's second Knife to deal with him. Move both bodies down the slope so that other soldiers don't spot them.

Now zoom out and press F11 to locate guards **B** and **C**. When guard **B** stands behind the biggest hut, with his back to the compound's entrance, walk calmly into the compound and kill him. Then pick off the other guard (**C**). There's another soldier patrolling outside the fence. Leave him for now.

Walk into the biggest hut, search the cupboard, and pick up the explosives. There is also a piece of the **bonus** picture. A prisoner is being interrogated in one of the nearby huts. Look through the doorway ([W]) to scout the situation. The room is split in two. Wait until the right half only has one guard, then sneak in and knife him. Knife the next guard as he returns. When dealing with the two remaining soldiers, knife the one holding the Rifle first. The other is unarmed and will only attack with his fists. Search the cupboard here to find another Knife and a piece of the **bonus** picture.

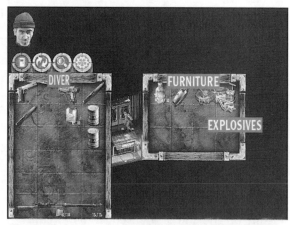

The explosives are located in the biggest hut. They're a special object, so any one of your Commandos can plant them.

The soldier on the bridge is a sniper. You'll need to kill him so you can safely access the prison compound below.

Give the extra Knife to the Green Beret. Leave the compound. Next move up behind the guard standing next to the metal crate near the railroad track. Kill him and dump his body in the nearby compound. Use the Thief to unlock the crate. You'll find Trip Wire, Wirecutters, a First Aid Kit, and another Knife.

Using either the Diver or Green Beret, walk along the bridge and kill the sniper standing at the first support. Make sure that you kill him when the man guarding Guinness (below) has his back to you. Move the sniper's body away from the edge so he won't be spotted.

Now you need to free Guinness ([A]). Move along the side of the buildings next to the railroad track and sneak past the gaze of guard [B] to reach the slope ([C]). Zoom out and focus on the lower village area. Several guards are on the first level, and an Officer who regularly walks down the stairway on an extended patrol. When the Officer starts this route—leaving building **A** to walk down the steps—you have time to take out the guards one by one. Let's start with the guard next to the hut (**E**).

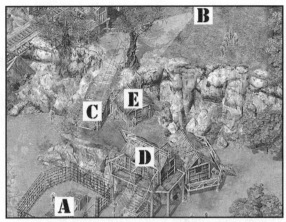

To free Guinness, you need to sneak past the guard (**B**), kill the soldiers at **C** and **D**, then eliminate the jailer at **A**. Tricky.

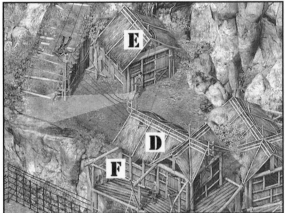

Use Cigarettes to lure the soldier away from building **E**. You're now free to approach building **D** and its guards.

Attract the guard standing next to the smaller hut (**E**) with Cigarettes. Kill him and hide his body behind the larger building (**D**). Wait for the Officer to return. When he starts his patrol again, quickly knife the guard (**F**) scanning the prison compound below. Move the body around the side of the large building (**D**) so that the Officer isn't alerted when he returns.

If there's a second guard on the walkway in front of building **D**, distract him with Cigarettes and kill him. Hide the body.

Look through the door near where you just killed guard **F**. Wait until the Officer in the room walks in to look out the window. Enter the room and kill him before he spots you. There are more guards in the room beyond, but you're hidden from their view. Simply walk in and kill them quickly using a Knife. The Green Beret is perfect for this operation. Note the radio—you'll need to use it later.

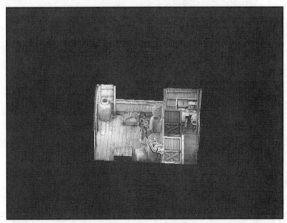

Take out the guards in building **D**. Note the radio here—you'll use it to call the train at the end of the mission.

Throw a packet of Cigarettes on the walkway to attract the attention of the patrolling Officer when he returns. Monitor the eyesight of the half-naked soldier (the Jailer) who's guarding Guinness in the compound below. Don't throw the Cigarettes where the Jailer can see them. For now we just want to lure in the Officer. When the Officer has been lured and killed, do the same for the patrolling Jailer. When you've silenced the Jailer, search him to find a set of keys.

Most soldiers can be distracted from their duties with a pack of Cigarettes. If this doesn't work, try a bottle of Wine.

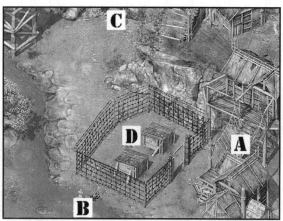

Crawl down the steps (A) to ensure that enemy soldiers don't spot you. Kill soldiers B and C before freeing Guinness.

Place a view marker (Tab) in the middle of the stairway (A) so you can see which guards regularly look at it. When nobody is looking, crawl down the steps and stand outside the building below. Lying low, deal with the guard (B) who's washing in the river. Hide his body.

Continue crawling around the edge of the prison compound until you can knife the guard (C) standing next to the bridge. Finally, move back to the compound and free Guinness (D).

Next, you want to go into the building opposite the prison compound. The keys you took from the Jailer will open the door, but walking through it sends you right into an enemy crossfire. Death will be swift and inescapable. Instead, work on getting rid of the guards that surround the building.

Monitor the vision of the guard close to the riverbank (**E**) and throw some Cigarettes at the limit of his vision—so you don't attract anybody else. Crawl around the semicircular guard post, knifing the sniper (**F**) in the window. Kill and remove the body of the soldier (**G**) guarding the door.

Kill all the guards patrolling outside the building here before you attempt to enter it.

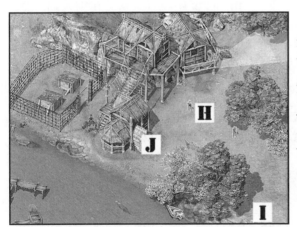

Lure the guard at **H who faces the river. Watch out for the soldier who patrols up and down the riverbank (**I**).**

Of the remaining guards, watch out for **H** and **I** (who patrols the riverbank toward the edge of the map). The other guards all have their backs to you. Distract and disable **H** and **I** using well-placed Cigarettes, before creeping up behind the other soldiers to kill them. When the guards in this area have been eliminated, move back to the building next to the river and enter it via door **J**.

Once inside the building, kill the Japanese soldiers there. Unlock the metal crate to find Wine, Sleeping Pills, a Trap, Wirecutters, Smoke Grenades, and a First Aid Kit. Make sure you take the Wine and Sleeping Pills. Next, go through the only other door and into the bottom level of the building—you should see the body of the dead sniper you knifed earlier. Combine the Sleeping Pills with the Wine and throw the poisoned bottle toward the Officer who's pacing around the room above. He'll spot the Wine and eventually drink it, sending him slumping unconscious to the floor. Climb the ladder and kill or knock out the remaining guards.

Guinness needs to inspect the model of the bridge so you can determine the best place to plant the explosives.

Take control of Guinness and guide him to the model of the bridge, using [Shift] to have him examine it. Search the box next to the model to find another **bonus** picture piece. Open your Notebook to check that you have completed all the major mission objectives. Send the Thief back across the river to ride the elephant if you haven't done so.

Set the explosives in the explosive Trap located on the bridge support. Think of it as an invisible piece of furniture.

Finally, move your squad back to the bridge, running past the prison compound and along the riverbank. Climb the ladder to get on the bridge itself and place the explosives— the trap needs to be set in the barrels in the center of the bridge. Examine and open the explosive Trap using [W]. There's also a **bonus** picture piece here. Once the explosives have been placed, send somebody to use the radio (located in the building above the prison compound). This signals the train and ends the mission.

MISSION SECRET

Bonus photo pieces required: 6

Once again, you find yourself on familiar ground—the guard post from the first Training Camp. This time, however, the mission takes place at night. As usual, you have been given the Sapper and the Thief to complete this mini-mission.

Start by knocking out the nearby guard when the patrolling guard walks away. Hide his body behind the bushes that screen your starting point from the guard post. Note where the patrolling guard shines his flashlight. Throw Cigarettes into his sight and wait until he picks them and turns to go back to his patrol route. Attack him from behind and stash his body behind the bushes.

This bonus mission is another variation on the first Training Camp mission. In short: find some Grenades and raise a little hell.

Take control of the Thief and go past the searchlights and up onto the telephone wires. Swing over to the far telephone pole (near the small bunker). Climb down when the patrolling guard below walks away from the pole. Crawl in between the two soldiers in the bunker and switch the searchlights off at the console. Next, crawl across to the metal crate and open it when the patrolling guard isn't looking. Take the Grenades, Wirecutters and the Flamethrower. Crawl back to the telephone wires and return to the Sapper. Give the Sapper the new equipment.

Take control of the Sapper and crawl towards the large bunker. Throw a Grenade into the bunker to kill the soldiers there. When other guards go to investigate, shoot the soldier at the guard post and then throw another Grenade at the guards who have gathered to look at their dead comrades. Cut through the wire fence near the bunker and shoot any enemy soldiers that remain.

CHAPTER 11

THE GUNS OF SAVO ISLAND

PRIMARY OBJECTIVES	SECONDARY OBJECTIVES
• Destroy the guns	• Contact the shipwrecked sailor
• Rescue the Allied pilot	• Steal the Golden Monkey
• Find the explosives	• Blow up the wall behind the Golden Monkey
• Escape in the seaplane	• Steal the key to the tunnels

WALKTHROUGH

In this mission you are assigned the Diver, Green Beret, Driver, and Sapper. You also have access to an extra character—Wilson, the shipwrecked sailor. This shaggy-haired castaway is more than just a sun-tanned wacko. He can perform much the same role here as Whiskey the Commando dog did in the Das Boot mission. Use him to distract guards, scout new locations, and carry items.

Your troops start in an inflatable dinghy off the coast of the island. Zoom out ([−]) and paddle your dinghy, staying away from the shore as much as possible, until you are opposite the beach (A). Head for the shore at B and talk to the shipwrecked sailor, Wilson. Once you've done this, you can take control of him just like any other Commando. Note the small beach at point C. This is where you'll head next.

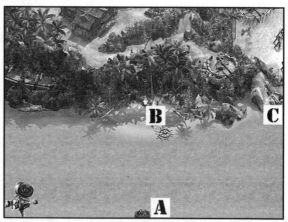

Paddle the dinghy along the bottom of the screen until you are opposite the beach (B). This is the safest way to get ashore unseen.

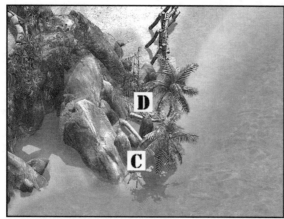

Controlling the Diver, crawl ashore at point C and move to a safe hiding place behind the rock at D. Stay low so the guards don't spot you.

Take control of the Diver and transfer the Green Beret's Knife to him so that he has two. Slowly swim toward point C on the next beach, keeping close to the rocks. If the soldier manning the big gun on the cliffs spots you, he'll radio the patrol boat that will come to investigate. If this happens before you've worked your way inland, you'll be mown down by the patrol boat's deck gun before you can even get off the beach. Crawl under the two palm trees and behind the large rock (D) that will block the enemy's view of you.

There are two soldiers you have to be concerned about on this beach. The first (E) walks back and forth along the length of this small bay. The other is one of two studying a small box further up the beach (F)—he regularly turns around to scan the ocean. Using the rock as cover, throw the pack of Cigarettes to lure in the beach-wandering guard (E).

Use Cigarettes to lure the guards at E and F within range of the Diver's Knife-throwing abilities.

Throw the Cigarettes just in front of the small rock on the shoreline. This keeps you hidden from the approaching guards.

To attract guard E, throw the Cigarettes just in front of the smaller rock. When the guard gets close enough, throw the Diver's Knife to kill him. The other guard (F) will either notice the dead body or you can lure him in using the Cigarettes again. Either way, kill him quickly with the second Knife.

Retrieve your weapons and crawl up the beach to knife the soldier next to the wooden box. Examine the box to get a Mine Detector and five anti-personnel Mines. Take control of the rest of your Commandos (and Wilson), and move them to the beach to join the Diver.

TIP

Make sure that you hide the bodies of any soldiers you knock out or kill. If the alarm is raised, you're unlikely to escape the island alive.

This beach is far from clear—one man still stands by the gun emplacement, and two soldiers guard the path to the next beach. There's also a path here that leads inland. The two soldiers guarding the beach never look at the gunner, so use the Diver and his Knife-throwing skills to kill him. Next, when the Officer has finished talking to the soldier guarding the exit to this beach, sneak up behind the soldier and use the Diver's Knife. You'll just have time to retrieve your blade and hide the body before the Officer returns. Repeat the process to get rid of the Officer.

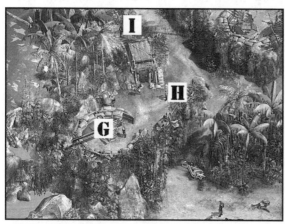

Take out the gun emplacement in three stages—the guard at **H**, followed by the soldiers at **G**. Then attack the men at **I**.

Take the path that leads up to the gun emplacement. The emplacement (**G**) is manned by three soldiers, only one of whom ever faces toward the path that you're using. Wait and watch—you'll see that an Officer (**H**) regularly makes the trip between this gun emplacement and a group of soldiers and sailors farther up the path (**I**). He is easily distracted by a well-thrown pack of Cigarettes, then silently killed by the Diver and dragged into the bushes. The Sapper has an extra Knife in this mission. Give it to the Green Beret.

Using the Green Beret, deal with the three soldiers around the gun emplacement in quick succession. Wait until the patrolling guard turns his back. Immediately stand and attack the guard as he walks away. Quickly knife the soldier with the Binoculars and then the gunner. There's a locked door here—you'll need a key.

Use Tab to monitor the vision of one of the sailors at **I**. Use the Cigarette trick, throwing them where the sailor can see them. This needs to be right on the very limit of his vision. Make sure

Throw the Cigarettes to attract the attention of the sailors stationed at I.

the Diver has two Knives. Kill the first sailor when he gets close enough, then quickly take out the second sailor who runs to examine the body. Remove the two bodies.

Now monitor the vision of the guard—he's hidden behind a rock. Throw the Cigarettes for him and use the Diver to kill him. The remaining Officer will see the body and run to investigate, allowing you get him with the Diver's second Knife. There's a wooden box here. Open it to find a Flamethrower and some Binoculars.

Make sure that you kill the guard on this high platform—he can see the entire compound from here.

For the next part of the island, you can take out all the enemies using just the Diver and the Green Beret. Crawl both men up the path toward the first bamboo buildings. Use the Green Beret to crawl up to the nearest guard who stands with his back to the path. Stab him and hide the body. Next, move him back down the path and along to a ladder leading to a tower. Climb the ladder and, staying low, knife the guard there. Move the Green Beret back to the top of the path.

In the village, crawl the Diver along the ground toward the nearby gun emplacement (**A**). Keep as close to the rocks as possible so the guard on the platform (**B**) doesn't spot you. The gunner at **A** has his back to you, so throw the Knife and kill him. Retrieve the Diver's Knife and use it to kill the guard standing on the raised wooden walkway (**B**).

Use the Diver's Grapple to climb up to the walkway to retrieve his Knife. There's a guard patrolling the front of the platform (**C**), plus a sniper on top of the building next to it (**D**). Don't attack the obvious guard. Instead, head through the doorway into the sniper's building. Immediately kill the guard inside, then search the cupboard for a **bonus** photo piece. Climb the ladder and kill or knock out the sniper.

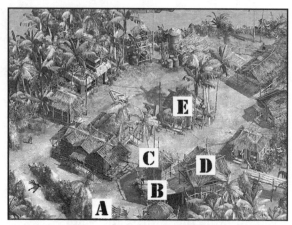

This village area may look daunting, but it can be neutralized using the Diver and the Green Beret.

Like the German soldiers in the previous missions, the Japanese army just can't get enough of imported Cigarettes.

Move the Diver back out of the sniper's building and back to the raised platform (**C**). Monitor the vision of the soldier outside hut **E**. Throw a pack of Cigarettes at the limit of his vision (near the bunker) and then throw a Knife at him once he's in range, collecting his Wirecutters when you're done. Now turn your attention to the guard on the raised platform (**C**). There's a patrolling guard who regularly comes close. Wait until he has walked away, then take out the guard and remove his body from view.

Draw the final patrolling guard away from his route—he walks to a position in front of the raised platform C, toward the wooden footbridge, through the building next to the footbridge, and back again. He can be lured away from this path and onto the raised platform using Cigarettes. The Diver simply needs to hide behind the hut and knife the soldier when he has picked up the Cigarettes and turns to walk away. His removal allows the Green Beret to enter the large building (F). The easiest way into this building (G) is via the doorway opposite the raised platform.

Inside the large building is an empty storeroom, occasionally visited by an Officer and a guard. You should be able to see the other guards in a nearby room. Peer through the doorway until you see the guard on his own and with his back to you. Sneak the Green Beret inside, stab him, and move the body outside. Do the same for the patrolling Officer.

Search the larger room next door to find a First Aid Kit. You should be able to sneak up behind the remaining soldiers to knock out them. Search the shelves in the smallest room to find a piece of the **bonus** picture.

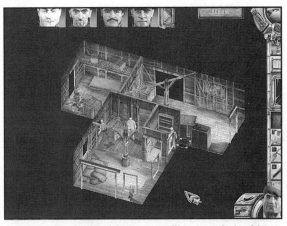

Once you've dealt with the patrolling guards in this building, the rest of the soldiers are easy to dispatch.

Surprisingly, you can throw a Grenade into a building (killing all inside) and nobody will notice the noise or fiery destruction.

Move to building H next to the bunker—this is a small barracks with five resting soldiers inside. Lure down the soldier on top of the bunker using the Cigarettes. Monitor his field of vision to see where to throw them. Next crawl up to the guard in front of the bunker and stab him. The door here leads down to the guns, but is locked. Moving on, take out the guard who's smoking at the back of building F.

Remove any dead bodies from open view. If the alarm is raised, you'll be dead in minutes. This area is almost clear, but be wary. The huts near the bridge hold four and two Japanese soldiers respectively, and there are five in hut **H** near the bunker. Toss a grenade at the one near the bunker first—the alarm won't be raised.

Before you blow up the huts near the bridge, you need to deal with the guard kneeling next to the river. Throw Cigarettes near the bridge (on your side) and use the Diver to knife the soldier lured by them. Or use two packets of Cigarettes, plus the Driver's Trip Wire strung across the pathway to knock out the soldier. Once he's been dispatched, you're clear to throw Grenades into the two buildings close to the river, killing those inside. You might, however, want to save your Grenades. These reservist soldiers won't come out unless the alarm is raised.

Use two packs of Cigarettes to lure enemy soldiers across the footbridge. Suckers!

Across the footbridge, several armed guards complicate your route to the Allied prisoner.

Across the footbridge, two Japanese soldiers are talking (**I**), and two more are guarding the Allied captive (**J**). There's also another one on the large wooden bridge (**K**). You can't cross this footbridge yet—a guard wandering near the Allied prisoner will spot you. To get rid of him, set the Trip Wire again, monitor his vision, and lure him across the bridge with the promise of Cigarettes. Use one pack to lure him across the bridge and another pack to guide him to the Trip Wire.

Now for the two guards on the bridge (**I**). Use the Driver to place a pack of Cigarettes near the steps leading to the raised platform, and another pack of Cigarettes in the middle of the bridge. Then place the Driver's Trip Wire right in front of the Cigarettes near the steps. Hide your team behind the hut next to the footbridge.

Take control of Wilson and run toward the two soldiers. The sound waves that this unkempt castaway generates will make the soldiers turn toward him. One guard will spot the Cigarettes on the footbridge and walk to them. When he's picked them up, he'll spot the second pack—but not the Trip Wire in front of it. When the soldier has been killed, reset the Trip Wire to work with the second guard.

Kill the enemy guards by luring them away from their positions with Cigarettes, straight into a leg-breaking Trap.

Cross the footbridge and knife the guard on the large wooden bridge. There's one guard left near the Allied prisoner and three stationed around the gun emplacement below. Take out the guard next to the captured prisoner using one of the Driver's Molotov Cocktails. Free the prisoner by holding the mouse cursor over the cage and pressing ⌈Shift⌋.

Leave the three guards below for now and move your team back to the beach.

With the Allied soldier free, you need to clear the second beach and locate the key to the tunnels. Without the key, you can't make your way into the subterranean complex to blow up the giant guns. First turn your attention to the two bunkers (**A**). The first leads into a cave that in turn leads up to the gun emplacement above **B**.

The second beach is lightly defended, but requires patience to conquer.

Note the guard opposite the bunkers at **C** and the gunner in the gun emplacement (**D**). Also, there are two guards standing near the wooden bridge (**E**), two more opposite them (**F**), and several soldiers near the beach (**G**). For now, however, head through the left doorway of the two bunkers at **A**.

Use Wilson to scout the left bunker at **A**. Throw a Grenade through the doorway to take out the two nearest guards. Bring in the Green Beret and the Driver. Drop the Green Beret to the ground near the crates and set him to provide Standing Coverage (**X**) up the passageway. This causes him to shoot the soldier working next to the wooden box.

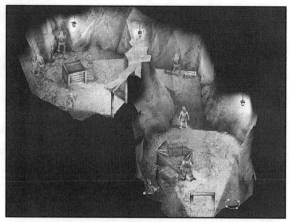

You can often get away with wild gunfire in enclosed spaces WITHOUT setting off a general alarm.

Select the Driver and throw a Molotov Cocktail when the remaining guards come to investigate. The Green Beret will take out the others with the Rifle. Open the wooden box here to find a Remote-Controlled Bomb and a Ladder.

Send the Green Beret through the only exit and out into the gun emplacement (**B**). Stab the nearest soldier, then lure the second away from his position with Cigarettes—make sure that you don't kill him too close to the final soldier or the gunner will hear his comrade's dying gurgles. Bring up the Diver to dispatch the gunner with a well-thrown Knife.

Make your way back down and into the second bunker. Wait until all three soldiers are in range, and then have the Sapper throw a grenade between them. Search the furniture in this room for two more Remote-Controlled Bombs, two Grenades, two Molotov Cocktails, and a piece of the **bonus** picture. You should now have three Remote-Controlled Bombs which you'll eventually use to blow up the three guns on this island.

TIP
Stay low at all times.
Minimize your exposure
to the enemy. What he
can't see, he can't shoot.

Now to cross the beach. Use the Diver to knife the soldier next to the rocks while he has his back to you. Next, crawl up to the gun emplacement (**D**), but don't kill the gunner just yet. He can be seen by one of the soldiers talking by the cargo net (**F**). Lure the keen-eyed soldier away toward the bunker using Cigarettes. Kill him, then kill the gunner in the gun emplacement.

Rotate the camera view until you can see the two guards talking by the wooden bridge (**E**). Monitor the vision of the one who looks at the gun emplacement. Use the Diver and Cigarettes to lure him away from his position and knife him. Take out the two remaining guards here—both should have their backs to you. Hide the bodies in the gun emplacement.

Three guards remain at **G**—one on the beach, the other two on a walkway that stretches out across the water. The soldier kneeling on the beach is easy to dispatch. Take control of the Diver and lure the patrolling guard that's pacing the walkway onto the land with Cigarettes—hide behind the cargo net and ambush him. Finally, crawl the Diver onto the walkway, monitor the last guard's field of vision, and approach when he looks through his Binoculars. Knife this last guard from distance.

When the soldiers on this second beach are eliminated, move your team to the cargo net. Climb the net when the patrolling guard (**H**) walks away on his patrol route to **I**. Kill the two men near the gun emplacement when their backs are to you, hiding their bodies behind the gun (**J**) so they can't alert the patrolling guard to your presence. Monitor the vision of the patrolling guard and kill him when he returns.

Three guards are in the building nearby (**K**). Leave them. You only need to get rid of the guard outside this

When the patrolling guard (**H**) walks away from the gun emplacement, quickly kill the two guards nearby.

building (**L**)—he's looking straight at the entrance to the Command Center (**M**). Use Wilson to distract him (with the Bugle), so you can step out and kill him with a Knife.

Next, go for the big gun emplacement (**I**). Creep up behind the gunner and knock him out—killing him will only alert the remaining solder. Knock out or kill the soldier with the Binoculars. Hide the bodies with the others (**J**).

Of the two green entrances (**M**), choose the bigger one. Go in with the Green Beret and stab the two men at the top of the shaft. When the lone soldier below has his back to you, climb down the ladder and kill him. Search the box to get two more Remote-Controlled Bombs.

Go into the second entrance (**M**) and into the room beyond. There are three guards here, but they won't see you as you stand at the end of this corridor. Deal with the two closest to you using a Molotov, and then shoot the last man as he investigates the charred corpses.

There are three doors here—two lead into the Command Center. The other (at the far end of the corridor) leads to a room where you'll find the Golden Monkey. There's also a grate in the floor leading to an underwater tunnel to the sea.

An Officer (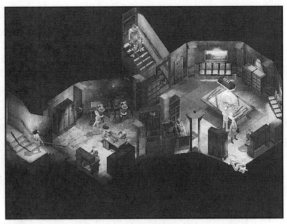) in the Command Center is holding the keys you need. The room is packed with enemy guards. Get the Sapper to lay down some Mines in front of the doorway opposite the Officer, then set up the rest of your squad to provide Standing Coverage auto-fire (X) aimed at the door. Send in the Green Beret to assassinate the Officer with a single Rifle shot. Run out of the room, retreat quickly behind your squad, and wait for the enemy troops to follow. The ones that don't get caught by the exploding Mine will be picked off by your men. When everyone is dead, search the Command Center for useful objects (including the key to the tunnels). You'll find three parts of the **bonus** picture here.

The dashing Officer in white holds the keys that will allow you access to the tunnels underneath the island.

The room at the end of the corridor contains the Golden Monkey. Only the Green Beret can lift this gilded ape head, but even he isn't strong enough to carry it up a ladder. Instead, use a Remote-Controlled Bomb to blow up the cracked wall here. Remember to leave the room before you detonate the bomb. After blowing your escape hole, leave the Golden Monkey where you found it. If you try to go through the hole now, you'll be spotted and shot by the soldiers guarding the nearby beach. First, you need to blow up the island's guns. The bunker you need is identified on your mission map—it's the locked door near where you freed the Allied soldier. Move your team back down the cargo net, across the beach, and through the cave to reach it.

The Golden Monkey is too heavy to carry out of the storeroom. You need to blow a hole through the wall to get it out.

Send Wilson ahead of you to scout the way. The first room contains two soldiers—you should be able to creep behind them to knock them out. Next, take the door directly opposite. The other one leads into a room where a group of Japanese soldiers are busy digging. There's a crate in here containing Grenades if you want to try your luck. If not, look through the door of the next room and enter when the guard walks away from you. Again, Knife skills will see you through. There's only one exit that opens out into a winding corridor dotted with strategically-placed crates.

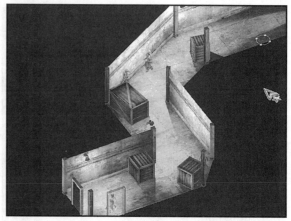

Use the large crates as natural cover to hide your team from the patrolling Japanese guards.

Make sure that the Diver has two Knives. Hide behind the nearest crate and, when the patrolling guard is farthest away, throw a Knife to kill the closest guard. When his compatriot comes to investigate, dispatch him with the second Knife. Quickly run and pick up your weapons, moving both of the bodies before the patrolling guard returns. Knife the last guard and move on.

The next room features two guards. Monitor the field of vision of the armed soldier and bring in the Diver to kill him. This attracts the attention of the second unarmed soldier. Rather than set the alarms off, he'll heroically try to knock you out. Knock him out and tie him up instead. The other doors here lead to barracks rooms and are filled with soldiers. Throwing Grenades will set off the alarms, so leave them alone.

Before you enter the gun room itself (via the steps), look through the door to watch the guard inside. Enter when he has his back to you. Kill him and the other guards here using Cigarettes and the natural cover available. Search the lockers near the elevator to find more Grenades, Molotov Cocktails, and two more **bonus** picture pieces. When the guards are dead or incapacitated, plant a Remote-Controlled Bomb next to each gun and leave the complex the way you came in. The door at the top of the elevator shaft can be opened only from the outside....

Plant a Remote-Controlled Bomb next to each of the three giant guns.

You need to clear the beach before you can safely enter the seaplane. All you'll need is a pack of Cigarettes and a Knife.

Now you need to plan your escape route. Move into a position where you can creep under the large wooden bridge toward the seaplane. Kill the guard (**A**) and hide behind the pile of supplies (**B**). Lure the guard standing on the wooden platform (**C**) with Cigarettes. Throw them in front of you so the guard doesn't spot the first guard you killed.

Deal with the guards on the beach near the supplies by simply attacking them from behind. The Diver is incredibly useful here. Finally, bring up the Driver to throw a Molotov at the two soldiers standing in front of the plane (**D**)—you need to kill them both at once or any survivor will raise the alarm.

Take out the remaining guards at the other end of the beach. Use the Diver to swim right around the plane so he can approach the guards without being spotted. Monitor the vision of the patrolling guard so you can approach the beach in safety. Knife both soldiers when their backs are turned. When the beach is clear, send the Green Beret through the hole in the cliff to grab the Golden Monkey. Move your team, including Wilson and the Allied prisoner you rescued, toward the plane.

Only the Green Beret is strong enough to carry the Golden Monkey to the seaplane.

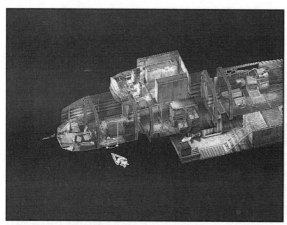

Use the Diver or Green Beret to kill the four-man crew of the seaplane, and the Driver to pilot the aircraft.

There are soldiers in the plane, but they can be picked off one-by-one by the Knife-happy Diver. Kill the soldier at the front of the aircraft, then attack the one at the back. Next, head down the ladder to attack the unarmed soldier below. Finally, deal with the last enemy on the flight deck.

Don't forget to set off the Remote-Controlled Bombs to destroy the guns before you all clamber on board. If you want to collect the final pieces of the bonus picture, you'll find them in the following areas: One is located in the building in the top-right corner of the upper screenshot on page 142. The other is in a room just before the gun room and is guarded by six soldiers in white overalls.

MISSION SECRET

Bonus photo pieces required: 10

The odds of completing this mission don't look good when you first begin. The Sapper has been captured by a German patrol and troops are fanning out to search the surrounding area. You need to rescue your brother-in-arms, break into the enemy outpost, and escape in a German truck. And if you could steal a Code Book while you're fighting the good fight, it will do wonders for the war effort. Or so they tell you. So where do you start?

Begin by selecting the Spy and slipping on his Lieutenant's Uniform. Walk up to the nearest German soldier and make him look the other way (press S, then Z). Take control of the Green Beret and crawl up to stab the soldier next to the wall. Monitor the vision of the soldier beyond so you're not spotted, then throw Cigarettes to lure in the soldier up ahead. Stab him and then kill the soldier who's distracted by the Spy.

It looks quiet now, but there are soldiers hiding behind the wall. Move the Spy to distract the soldier next to the telephone pole. Make him look anywhere but at the wall the Green Beret is hiding behind, then set the Green Beret to provide Standing Coverage (X) with the Machinegun through the gap between the wall and trees. Bring up the Driver and throw a Molotov Cocktail over the wall to kill the soldier hiding there. This will attract the soldiers who will be shot by the Green Beret. Get the Driver to throw extra Molotovs if things seem to be going badly.

Wait for the troops to move into their defensive positions—you don't want to encounter any soldiers on the move.

Send the Spy down to free the Sapper. Jab the three soldiers that remain with the Syringe and tie them up when they drop unconscious. Free the Sapper. Next, move all members of your squad to the thick wall that divides the map in two. Send the Green Beret into enemy territory using the telephone wire. Kill the unarmed soldiers near the truck and search the two wooden crates to find Wirecutters, a Ladder, and the Mine Detector. Return to the wall again, but drop down on top of it. Use the Ladder and drop it down over the side for the other Commandos to use. The Sapper also has a Ladder in his inventory. Use this on the other side of the wall.

The soldiers working near the wire fence are all unarmed. They generally won't raise the alarm if they spot you.

Give the Wirecutters and Mine Detector to the Sapper. Cut the wire fence and use the Mine Detector to locate the Mines. Defuse the Mines you find and cut the fence again to move up behind the truck. If the truck is destroyed, you'll fail the mission. Make sure one of your Commandos has a Machinegun with lots of ammunition. Aim at the enemy soldiers and press X to put the Commando on autofire. The enemy won't stand a chance. Simply get into the truck and drive it offscreen to complete the mission.

CHAPTER 12

THE GIANT IN HAIPHONG

PRIMARY OBJECTIVES	SECONDARY OBJECTIVES
• Contact the Sapper and the Thief	• Talk with the shopkeeper
• Find the explosives	• Rescue Natasha
• Destroy the large fuel tanks	• Hide inside the truck
• Destroy the small fuel tanks	
• Infiltrate the aircraft carrier	

MISSION WALKTHROUGH

Your first priority is to free your comrades—the Sapper and Thief. Natasha is also hidden on this map. Talk to the shopkeeper to find out where she is. Find her a suitable disguise so she can walk around the dock area unnoticed.

Walk right from your starting position, without rotating the screen. Note the patrolling guard (A). When this guard isn't looking, hide beside the small building (B). Stab the guard when he returns and hide his body while searching him for a Rifle. Enter building B and kill the three soldiers inside using the Knife. The two wooden boxes here contain a First Aid Kit, Wine Bottle, and a Machinegun. Head outside and use the Wine to lure the guard standing next to building B. After you've killed him, hide his body in building B and steal the dead guard's Rifle and Cigarettes.

You never have enough firepower at the start of a mission. Make it your priority to steal some bigger, better weaponry.

The first part of this mission involves little more than a Knife and a packet of Cigarettes. Don't leave home without them.

Now return to your starting point. Creep up behind the enemy guard next to building C and kill him when the guard standing opposite (D) isn't looking. Crawl across the street between buildings C and E and creep up behind guard D. Kill him only when no other guards are nearby. Quickly pick up his body and carry it back to the starting point. Storm the building half-covered with trees (E), stabbing its inhabitants before they can fight back. Bust into building C, killing the two soldiers inside and picking up your first bonus picture piece from the cupboard. A crate here contains a pack of Cigarettes and Binoculars.

Cross the street again between buildings C and E and move up next to the wall of building F. Distract the soldier who patrols in front of this building (G) with Cigarettes. When you've killed him, carry his body into one of the buildings near the start point. Lure the second guard (H) away by throwing the Cigarettes into the middle of the street. Monitor the guard's vision (Tab) to see where to throw them. There's nothing of interest in building F. Walk up to building I next to it—there's a man painting the outside wall. Go through the door.

From your start position, aim for building I on your way to a rendezvous with the shopkeeper.

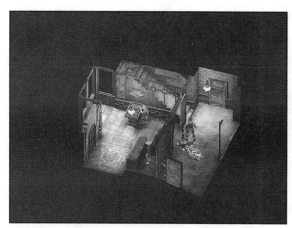

Use F10 to highlight doorways and pieces of furniture that contain useful items.

You can kill the first guard in the corridor. Lure the next soldier out of the nearby room with Cigarettes. The last soldier, sitting at the table, is a Grenadier. Leave him alone and move through the door opposite the one that you entered. This door opens into a corridor, which in turn leads to a storeroom. Kill the guard then search the wooden box for Sleeping Pills. Head up the stairway next to the storeroom. The room at the top is full of searchable furniture. Deal with the guards first and then pick up a First Aid Kit, Timed Bomb, two **bonus** picture pieces, and some Grenades.

Lie prone in this room and look through the door next to the filing cabinet. Open the door and knife the soldier on the balcony. His death attracts the attention of another soldier across the street. Stay on the balcony and lie in wait for him. Kill the guard when he arrives. That's two fewer enemies to worry about.

Head back downstairs and into the storeroom. Look through the doorway to see a guard standing outside a small green-roofed building. Nobody else can see him, so sneak out, stab him, and hide his body in the storeroom. Return to the small, green-roofed building and hide in front of its entrance.

Use view markers to determine whether an enemy can see a specific location (for example, this guard).

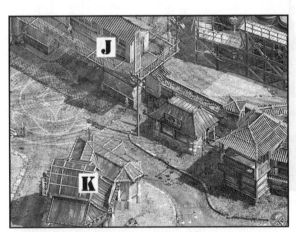

The shopkeeper knows where Natasha can be found. Find him inside building K.

Place a view marker in the middle of the street so you can see who is likely to spot you when you run across it. Zoom out the view (–) to see a few guards walking on a metal balcony (J) above the gateway to the docks. Cross the street toward building K only when these two guards are *not* looking your way. Move across to the small circle of children.

You should be safe behind this building (**K**). The five-man patrol regularly wanders the streets nearby. A soldier is also stationed on almost every street corner. You need to get inside the building you are hiding behind **K**. The double doors opposite the green-roofed building provide the only entrance. Time your move when the five-man patrol has passed and the men on the metal walkway are looking the other way.

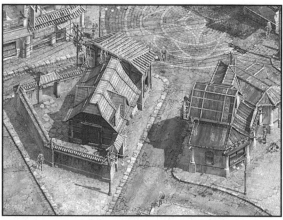

Zoom out and study the soldiers' movements, especially the five-man patrol.

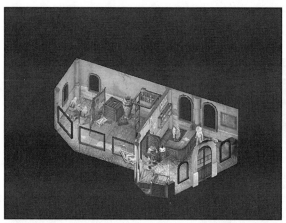

Talk to the shopkeeper and search the shelves behind the bar to find a piece of the **bonus** photograph.

Once inside building **K**, talk to the shopkeeper. He tells you that Natasha is also being held in town. Check the shelves above the shopkeeper's counter to find a **bonus** picture piece. A screen in the next room hides several soldiers, while a restless guard moves around the room. When he walks away from the door, knock him out and tie him up (it won't make as much noise). Search the wooden box for some Oriental Clothes and a Sniper Rifle. Check the shelf for another First Aid Kit. Climb the ladder, stab the soldier, and search the furniture for another **bonus** picture piece. Climb back down and leave the building via one of the back windows.

Natasha is in building L. Make your first target the soldier on the street corner (M). Kill him only when the patrol has passed and the soldier (N) walking in front of building you are hiding behind is facing away from you. Hide the body behind the building. Monitor the vision of guard (N). When he's not looking, walk across the street and into the walled compound opposite (O). Quickly head into the doorway. Check the wooden box for extra supplies. Open the doorway into the next room and move to the side before you are spotted. Lure out the guard inside the room with Cigarettes and kill him. Search the chest he was guarding to find more Grenades.

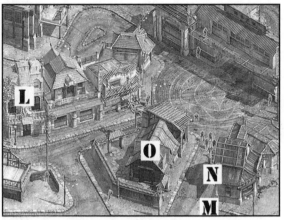

Knowing Natasha is in building L is one thing, but getting over to building L is quite another.

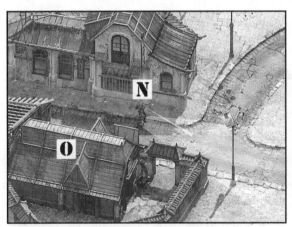

Eliminate the guards one-by-one as you head from the back of building K to the target building (L).

Drop prone and leave the building—the last room is too well defended for now, but a **bonus** picture piece is there so you'll go back later. Crawl back toward the street where the guard (N) paces up and down in front of the shopkeeper's building. Wait for the patrol to pass and lure him out of position with Cigarettes. Stab him and hide his body behind the shopkeeper's building with the others. Wait until the patrol passes again and move back to your earlier position in the walled compound (O).

Wait until the patrol passes again, and then creep up to the wall, intent on getting the guard (P) standing outside the walled compound. Attack him only when the guard (Q) walking on the raised green area is facing away from you. Again, when guard P is dead, dump his body behind the shopkeeper's building with the others.

Next, lure guard R away from the raised green area he's standing next to. Start as before by moving to a position outside the walled compound when the patrol passes. Lure guard R toward you using Cigarettes, but only when guard

The five-man patrol is formidable but slow moving. Attack guards P, Q, and R once the patrol has walked past your hiding place.

Q on the raised green area walks away. Hide the body of R behind the shopkeeper's building. Repeat the process for guard Q on the raised green area, except, since the angle is wrong for you to attack him, wait until he's picked up the Cigarettes and turned to walk back before you strike. You should have just enough time to grab the body and head for the green-roofed building. Dump the body and hide behind the wooden box (S).

The Green Beret could kill everyone in the town with just a Knife and some Cigarettes. But to get to the docks, you need Natasha.

When you are outside the green-roofed building, knock out the man near the truck. Tie him up and move under the gaze of the guard on the balcony. Move to the brown-roofed building at the end. Enter this building and kill the two guards in the two rooms here. This place proves useful for dumping dead enemy soldiers. Head back outside and stand at the back of the building. Lure in the nearest patrolling soldier using Cigarettes. Attract the sailor away from his position in the same way.

Walk to the side of the target building when the soldier stationed on the roof of the warehouse nearby can't see you. The safest way in is via the ladder here. Again, climb it only when the guard on the roof of the warehouse is looking away. Go through the doorway at the top. In the following room, lure out the guard who faces the corridor you started in. Knock him out and tie him up. Next, knock out and tie up the two remaining soldiers. Climb down the ladder to find Natasha, talk to her, and then give her the Oriental Clothes and the Sniper Rifle. Leave the building the way you came in.

To gain access to building **L**, climb up the ladder at the back. Watch out for the guard on the warehouse roof opposite.

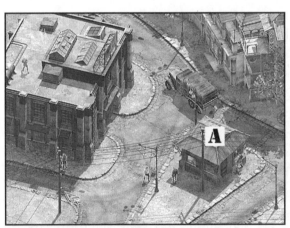

Kill the soldier inside building **A**. Use this place as a dumping ground for enemy guards that you eliminate.

When the guard on the warehouse isn't looking, move Natasha and the Green Beret down the ladder to street level. Move them behind the small hut (**A**) opposite the warehouse. To create an escape route for the Thief and the Sapper who are being held in the warehouse, eliminate the soldiers that surround it. Move Natasha into hut **A** and have her distract the soldier there. Use the Green Beret to kill him. When it's empty, this room serves as a great place to hide dead bodies.

Send Natasha up the ladder to the roof of the warehouse. Shoot the guard patrolling the roof—Natasha can't wear her disguise and fire the Sniper Rifle at the same time. Quickly shed the disguise, fire a killing shot, and press D to don the Oriental Clothes again. While you are up here, crawl across the roof and shoot the guard patrolling the balcony (B) on the building opposite the warehouse. Wait and shoot a second guard who comes to investigate the death of the first. This enemy previously guarded the side entrance to the warehouse.

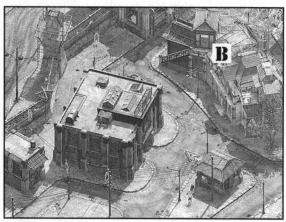

Use Natasha's skill with the Sniper Rifle to assassinate the guard patrolling the balcony at B.

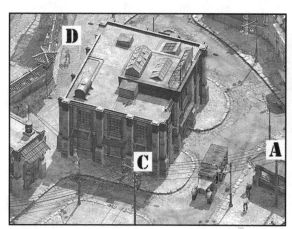

Before you enter the warehouse, eliminate the guards that patrol the perimeter.

Use Natasha to distract the soldier (C) patrolling the side of warehouse. Make sure he is facing away from building A. Knock out and tie up the men standing next to building A. Knock out the man in white first—punching these soldiers is quieter than stabbing them. Next, cross the street and kill the soldier (C), who is currently distracted by Natasha. Finally, Distract and kill the guard (D) who patrols the area directly behind the warehouse. Hide his body out of sight near the body of soldier C.

Move Natasha to the truck (**E**). Drive the truck to the side entrance of the warehouse (**F**). Send Natasha into the warehouse to free the Sapper and Thief. Once they are released, use Natasha to distract the guard who stands outside the room where the Sapper and Thief are. When this guard's back is turned, move the Thief and the Sapper out of the side entrance. Use Natasha to search the furniture in warehouse to find two **bonus** picture pieces, a Ladder, Grenades, a First Aid Kit, and some Binoculars.

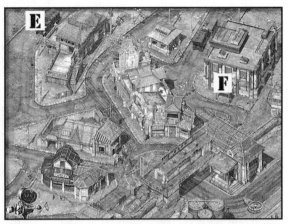

If you can hide in the back of the moving truck, do so. If it stops for any reason, use Natasha to steal the truck at **E**.

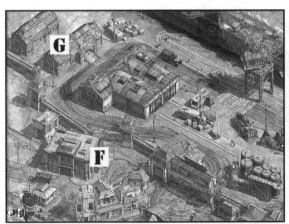

If Natasha (wearing her disguise) is driving the truck, the other Commandos can hide unseen in the back.

Move Natasha out of the warehouse side entrance and into the driver's seat of the truck and move the remaining Commandos into the back. With Natasha driving, her disguise extends to any passengers that she carries. This means that the Thief, Sapper, and Green Beret can hide in the truck. Take control of Natasha and drive the truck from **F**, through the gates of the dock, and around to park at **G** between the two buildings on the map's edge.

Take control of the Green Beret and knock out the soldier (**H**) standing outside the far building. Bring up the Sapper, then look through the doorway (**W**) to see the soldiers inside. Throw a Grenade into the building to take them out. Send Natasha in next to distract any soldiers that remain. Send in the Green Beret to kill any survivors. Finally, take control of the Thief and use him to unlock and open the two metal crates here. Take the three Remote-Controlled Bombs and the two Timed Bombs.

Park between the two buildings at the map's edge. Stab the guard and throw a Grenade into the building he was standing outside to kill the soldiers inside.

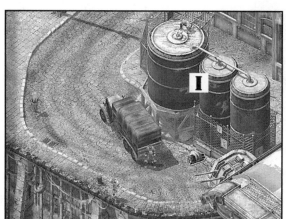

Place one of the Remote-Controlled Bombs at the base of the small fuel tanks. The explosion destroys them.

Move Natasha back into the truck (as the driver). When she is in the driver's seat, move the rest of the squad into the back of the vehicle. Drive across the base to the small fuel tanks (**I**). Gently nudge the truck next to the aircraft carrier as you pass. This causes the two soldiers working on it to stop what they are doing and move away—make sure that they move to the side of the large building opposite the carrier. When you eventually reach **I**, back up to the tanks in the truck and quickly plant one of the Remote-Controlled Bombs next to them.

Next, drive to the larger fuel tanks (J) and plant another Remote-Controlled Bomb at K when the guards on the balcony (L) and the patrolling soldier at M aren't looking. If you are spotted, quickly dive inside the truck to escape any guards that run to investigate. When the charges are placed, drive back to position G and detonate the charges.

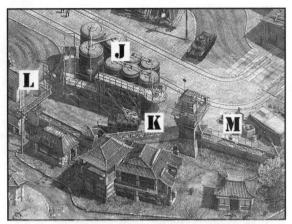

Plant the second Remote-Controlled Bomb at K, making sure the soldiers at L and M do not spot you.

To get onto the aircraft carrier, climb up the crane on the side of the dock. This is easier said than done.

Now move across the dock toward the crane. First, use Natasha to distract guard N near the supplies, making him look away from your current position. Use the Green Beret to stab soldier O outside the building where you obtained the explosives. Next kill the distracted guard (N). Now use Natasha to distract the sailor (P) standing outside the large building opposite. Move the Green Beret across to a position behind the supplies and stab the patrolling guard (Q) when his back is turned.

Plant a Remote-Controlled Bomb between the supplies and the side of the aircraft carrier. Move the Green Beret back behind one of the buildings and use the Sapper to throw a Grenade at the sailors hiding in the center of the supplies. This explosion may attract a tank that patrols the base. Zoom out and watch to see if it approaches. If it does, wait until it drives over the Remote-Controlled Bomb and then detonate it. If it doesn't investigate, simply carry on.

Explosions attract the attention of the small tank that patrols the base. Destroy it with your last Remote-Controlled Bomb.

Use one of the trucks to block the enemy's line of sight. This makes your approach to the crane easier.

Use the Green Beret to shoot the distracted sailor (**P**). Nobody is close enough to hear the gunshot. Hide the body near your truck. Next, use Natasha to drive the second truck in front of the two guards now sitting at **R**. These are the soldiers who were working on the truck earlier. Moving the truck blocks the view these soldiers have of guard **S** stationed on the dock. Use Natasha to distract guard **S**. Switch control to the Green Beret and stab guard **S**, hiding his body behind the supplies.

Use Natasha to distract guard 🝗 standing outside the large building. Take control of the Green Beret and stab soldier 🝖, who's guarding a pile of crates near the crane. Once he is dead, move across and knife guard 🝗. Use Natasha to drive the truck blocking the guards at 🝥 *over* the guards at 🝥. Nobody should be near enough to spot this maneuver. When they are dead, take control of the Green Beret and stab the soldiers inside the container (🝦).

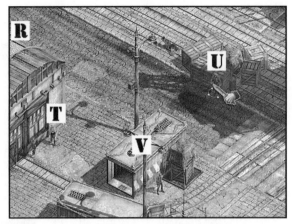

Before you can climb the crane, eliminate those guards that can see the ladder you'll be using.

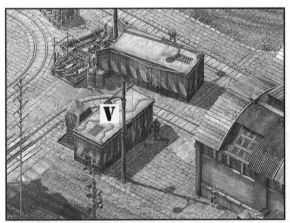

Use the Green Beret's Decoy to lure the stubborn guard 🝦 away from his position.

Locate the soldier standing guard in front of the container (🝦). Plant the Green Beret's Decoy behind the container and hide around the corner. Activate the Decoy to lure the soldier away from his position—he can see the crane and needs to be eliminated. When the soldier nears the Decoy, switch it off. As the soldier turns his back to examine the Decoy on the ground, creep up behind him and kill him. Move Natasha back into the first truck. Move the other Commandos into the back and drive the truck toward the crane.

Park the truck underneath the crane. Take control of the Sapper and press X to make him leave the vehicle. Prime a Grenade and throw it in the middle of the men standing on the dock. Quickly, move the Sapper back into the truck and wait while the Japanese soldiers search the blast area. Once the other soldiers have examined the dead bodies, they disappear. Keep hidden until things have returned to some semblance of normality. Note, however, that patrols are on heightened alert.

Park the truck directly underneath the crane and use the Sapper to throw a Grenade at the soldiers on the dock.

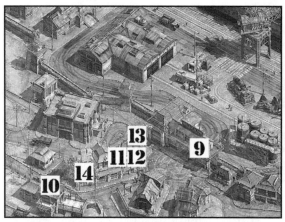

To access the **bonus** mission, you need to find the remaining **bonus** photo pieces indicated on this map.

If you want to access the **bonus** mission, this is the perfect time to find the final six remaining pieces of the **bonus** photograph. As you approach the end of the mission, you are better equipped to storm the buildings where the other **bonus** pieces are located. Eight of the 14 pieces have been highlighted in this walkthrough. The locations of the missing six (located mostly in cupboards) are shown here. When you've finished, drive the truck back and park it underneath the crane again.

Using the Sapper again, throw a Grenade to kill the sniper on the aircraft carrier. Take control of the Thief and guide him out of the truck and up the ladder on the crane. Climb up onto the gantry and move along it over the deck of the aircraft carrier. When you get to the end, right-click to drop from the crane onto the deck. Hold [Shift] and click on the long ladder on the aircraft carrier to drop it down to the dock. Shoot the nearby guard (use the Sniper Rifle) and move your Commandos up the ladder and onto the aircraft carrier. Enter the open container to complete the mission.

Only the Thief can climb across the crane and onto the aircraft carrier's deck. Drop the Ladder down for the others to climb.

MISSION SECRET

Bonus photo pieces required: 14

This **bonus** mission takes place on the *Shinano* once it has set sail. Your orders are simple: Sabotage the rudders on the Japanese Zeros so they can't fly (use Wirecutters), radio the position of the carrier to the Allies, and then escape in the two white prototype aircraft. Simple? No, not exactly.

Use the Driver to throw a Gas Grenade at the nearby sailor. Toss a Molotov Cocktail at the soldier who comes to investigate, killing both men. Move the Driver up the ladder and into a position where he can throw a Molotov Cocktail at the three men in the center of the deck. Wait until three more

While it's fairly easy to disable the green Japanese Zeros, you have to struggle getting into the radio room.

soldiers come to investigate the bodies, then launch the final Molotov Cocktail at them. Use the Green Beret to stab any soldiers that remain in this area. Still using the Green Beret, crawl along deck. Knock out and tie up two men near one of the other planes. Move down and distract and disable the armed soldiers working on the next plane. Open the wooden box to get some Wirecutters. Dispatch the guards near the remaining three planes, and then disable their rudders using the Wirecutters.

Extra ammunition (mostly Molotovs and Gas Grenades) is contained in wooden boxes scattered across the carrier. Rifles are in the metal crates. Work your way toward the aircraft carrier's radio room. Head toward the bow of the carrier via the boxes at Ⓐ and Ⓑ. Disable the final two aircraft at Ⓒ, before sneaking past the guards toward the metal crate at Ⓓ. The only access to the inside of the aircraft carrier is via the walkway at Ⓢ. This leads to a ladder, which in turn leads to Ⓢ. The door that leads inside the carrier is on this level. Kill every guard you encounter, then use the radio and escape in the aircraft.

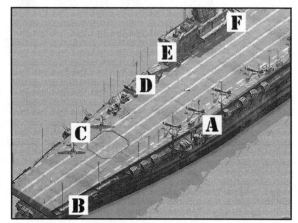

Reaching the wooden crates rewards you with more Gas Grenades and Molotov Cocktails.

CHAPTER 13

SAVING PRIVATE SMITH

PRIMARY OBJECTIVES

- Heal Private Smith
- Steal the Radio Codes from the safe
- Use Private Smith to radio HQ

SECONDARY OBJECTIVES

- Free the Green Beret
- Save the Sapper
- Rescue the Sniper

MISSION WALKTHROUGH

Saving Private Smith is a search-and-rescue operation. Although you can control the Sapper, the Green Beret, and the Sniper, the enemy has captured these three Commandos. The only free character at the start of this mission is the Thief—he's not much good in a fight, but his climbing abilities prove vital here. You can't rescue Private Smith unless you rescue your comrades.

Starting by the wreckage of the crashed plane, the Thief needs to rescue his comrades—the Green Beret, Sapper, and Sniper. Locate the Officer on the balcony of the nearby building. Monitor his vision ([Tab]). When he isn't looking (i.e., when he walks away from the green door), run to the wall of the town so you are standing directly below the building. Climb up to look through the small window above the balcony. Don't begin your ascent to the window until the guard on the balcony walks past post [A] to stand at [B]. Look through the window using [W].

Climb up the building here only after the guard has walked past point [A] toward [B]. Your destination is the small window above.

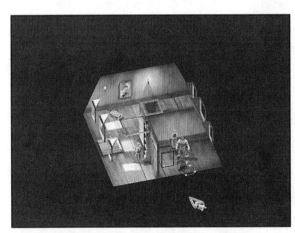

Use the Thief to knock out the soldier guarding the Green Beret. But use the Green Beret to tie up the unconscious guard.

The Green Beret is in the room here, guarded by a single Lieutenant. When the soldier has his back to the window, right-click to stop looking through the window and hold [Shift] to go through. Stand behind the Lieutenant and knock him out with a punch ([Q]). Quickly free the Green Beret. Take control of the Green Beret and tie up the unconscious Lieutenant before he wakes. Open the door and knock out the next guard. Tie him up and move the body into the room with the Lieutenant. Take the guard's Rifle. Finally, search the wooden box to find the Green Beret's favorite toys— Knife, Pistol, Cigarettes, and the Decoy.

Keeping control of the Green Beret, look out of the middle window opposite the room you were just in. Note the telephone wires. Use [Shift] to move the Green Beret across the wires to the next house (the one with the small garden). Thankfully none of the German soldiers look up.

Look out of the window ([W]) and note the telephone wires. The Green Beret and the Thief can climb across them.

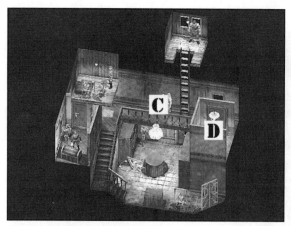

The Sapper is being held in the small room ([D]) at the end of the corridor.

In the next house, stay away from the trapdoor in the floor—the soldiers downstairs may spot you. A soldier below regularly runs between the two levels of the building below. Wait until this soldier moves down to the ground floor before climbing down the ladder and knifing the soldier ([C]) standing next to it. Quickly pick up the dead body and carry it into the small room ([D]) where the Sapper is being held. Close the door so you're not spotted when the patrolling soldier returns. Free the Sapper by holding [Shift] and clicking on him. Take control of the Sapper and search the murdered guard to recover the Mine Detector and a Mine.

Take control of the Green Beret again. Wait until the patrolling guard is outside the door with his back to you. Open the door and knife him. Search the dead soldier to get a Machinegun. Pick up the dead soldier and carry him over to the other room on this level—it contains two Germans and a large chest. Drop the body on the floor opposite the stairway and as close to the back wall as possible. Stand to the left of the room's door and knock on it using ⟨Q⟩. When the first German comes out to investigate (and spots the dead body), knife him. Repeat the process to dispatch the second soldier.

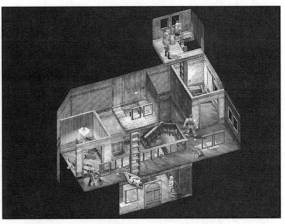

Use unconscious soldiers and dead bodies to attract the enemy soldiers' attention.

Head downstairs to kill the guards on the lower level. Always clear a house of men. If you leave them alive, they may attack you later.

Take out the remaining men on the top floor. Search the bodies to find a Sniper Rifle and more ammunition. Move down the stairway and, by monitoring the vision of the soldier standing below, creep up and knife him. Search his body for more ammunition for the Rifle you picked up earlier. Next, creep up behind the remaining soldier and kill him. Search the furniture and the wooden box to find a First Aid Kit, Grenades, another Pistol, Wirecutters, a Ladder, and some Cigarettes. You also find a piece of the bonus picture. Give the Grenades to the Sapper.

You can't just walk out of this house—the streets are crawling with German soldiers and the door is locked. Instead, send the Green Beret back across the telephone wires and back to the first building (where the Thief still waits). In this building, climb the ladder to the level above and knife the two guards there. Return to the room below. Use [W] to look through the trapdoor ([E]) in the floor. In the room below, there are two soldiers you can see, and several that you can't. Position the Green Beret to automatically cover the trapdoor with the Machinegun ([X]). To entice the soldiers, give the Thief a Pistol and have him fire off a shot. The Green Beret should be able to kill most of the soldiers that appear.

Gunshots alert any soldiers within earshot. Sometimes you can use this to your advantage.

Search the empty second floor of this building for useful items and bonus photograph pieces.

The house below should be empty of soldiers now. Press [F10] to highlight furniture that can be searched. There are some Binoculars in the large bedroom, some Sniper Rifle ammunition, and two pieces of the **bonus** photo in the other rooms here. A stairway leads down to the ground floor where several enemy soldiers wait to ambush the overconfident soldier. Leave it for now and look through the door in the bedroom. You see the guard on the balcony that you climbed past earlier. Send the Green Beret out to kill him. Use the Thief's Ladder to provide the Green Beret with a safe route to ground level.

There's a single soldier to the side of the building (beneath the telephone wires). Lure him toward the railings with Cigarettes and knife him. You can't get any farther until you clear the ground floor of this building. Use the Thief to look through the window on the side of the house where you used the Ladder (watch out for the eagle-eyed guard patrolling the green steps across the square). When the soldier inside has his back to you, send the Thief through the window to open the door from the inside. Now send in the Green Beret to do the killing.

The Green Beret can use Rifles, Pistols, and Machineguns, but his most effective weapon is the Knife.

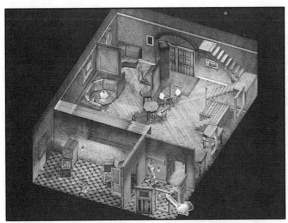

Head into the ground floor of the building. Search the guard in the storeroom to find a Blowtorch.

Several enemies lurk on the ground floor of this building. Distract and disable those you can't sneak up on. Search the bodies to find a Blowtorch and some Machinegun ammo. Search the cupboards behind the bar to find Wirecutters. Next, send the Thief across the telephone wires to the house where you freed the Sapper. Use him to unlock the ground floor door. Take control of the Sapper and look through the door using W.

The Sapper can see a Lieutenant (F) on the grass outside, a soldier in the bunker (G), and a patrolling guard (H) who regularly walks up and down the street that runs along the map's edge. When the patrolling guard (H) is busy in the town square, move the Sapper out the door and knock out the Lieutenant (F). Tie him up and drag him inside. Take care of the patrolling guard (H). Now only the soldier in the bunker (G) remains. Shoot him. Before you can move freely around on this side of the river, eliminate the guards stationed in the square.

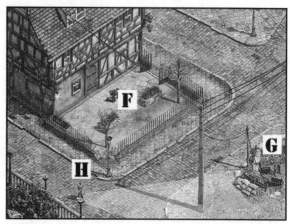

From his hiding place in this house, the Sapper can strike at the Lieutenant (F), the soldier (G), and the guard (H).

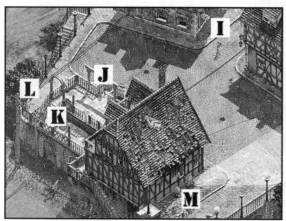

Zoom out to get a tactical view of the square. Eliminate all of the guards before you can free the Sniper.

Several guards need to be killed in this square. The closest soldier (I) patrols in front of the two buildings you already cleared. Across the street, soldier J commands a view of the whole square, while troops L and K also guard the area around the green wooden building. On the opposite side of this building (M), several soldiers guard the end of the bridge. Other soldiers look out of the building—one gazes across the river, one looks across the square, another stands in a window at M.

Guide the Green Beret (with a full Rifle) into the house where you found the Sapper. Move him up to the window where you killed the sniper and look through the window (**O**) to get a view across the square. Shoot the soldier (**I**) who patrols the front of the building. His death lures across soldier **J**—shoot him too. This soldier's death attracts soldier **K** and the soldier who was watching the square from the window of the green wooden building. Shoot both of these guards too. Finally, move the Green Beret from his firing position across the square to stab soldier (**L**). Watch out for the guard patrolling the steps at the back of the green wooden building.

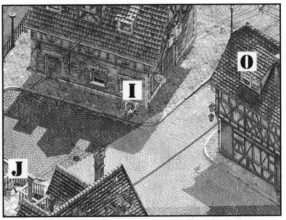

Shoot soldier (**I**) to attract the attention of the other soldiers guarding the green wooden building.

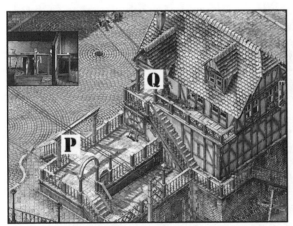

Approach the green wooden building via the steps at **P**. Use the Thief and his Ladder to provide access to the doorway (**Q**).

Search the bodies for ammunition. With the square cleared, approach the third house (where the Sniper is being held captive) from the green wooden steps (**P**). For now, only the Thief can climb up to the door at (**Q**). To enable the rest of your team to follow him, drop a Ladder over the side. If you haven't got a spare, run back to the bar and pick up the Ladder you used there. Once this is in place, position the Thief and the Green Beret on the balcony. If the guard patrolling the stairway that leads down to the river is still alive, use the Green Beret and quietly knife him.

Look through the first set of windows to see the guard patrolling the stairway inside this building. When the guard begins to move down the stairway, send the Thief through the window to unlock the door—he's the only one small enough. When the door is unlocked, take control of the Green Beret, enter the building, and dispatch the guard. Knife the second soldier, who you see kneeling at a downstairs window. Next pick up and drop a dead body within sight of the doorway that leads to the other rooms. Stand to the left of the doorway and press Q to knock on it. This lures out one soldier who runs to examine the dead body. Kill him quietly.

Take care of the men on the lower level before you turn your attention to those soldiers guarding the battered Sniper.

The Sniper has to make do with a German Sniper Rifle. Obtain as much ammo for it as you can.

The rest of the soldiers won't fall for this trick. Knock out the Officer in the next room when he has his back to you—it's quieter than stabbing him. Knife the sniper at the window and steal his Sniper Rifle. Finally, sneak into the remaining room and stab the guard torturing your Sniper. Free the Sniper. Equip your Sniper with the Sniper Rifle. Search all available furniture. You find some Sniper Rifle ammunition and a **bonus** photo piece in the cupboard. Find another **bonus** photo piece and some more Binoculars in the chest of drawers on the lower level.

Using the Green Beret and the Sapper (one equipped with a Machinegun, the other with a Rifle), locate the trapdoor on the ground floor. Position the Commando with the Machinegun facing the trapdoor and use $\boxed{X}$ to specify a field of fire that covers it. Position the Sapper so he can also aim at the trapdoor. Both Commandos should lie prone. Using the Sapper, fire off a shot to attract the attention of the soldiers below. As the three soldiers come up, the Green Beret can mow them down. As usual, search the bodies for extra items and ammunition.

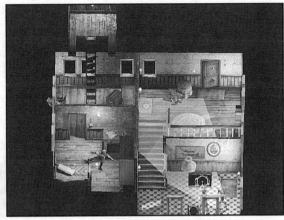

Lure out the soldiers hiding in the basement by using the same Machinegun trap you used earlier.

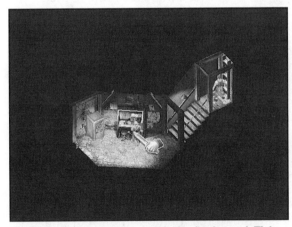

Go down the trapdoor and stab the final guard. The radio is here. Now you need to rescue Private Smith.

Send the Green Beret down into the room below to kill the remaining soldier with his Knife. Use the Thief to open the safe here and get the Radio Codes inside. Note the radio here. Bring Private Smith here after you have rescued him—he needs to operate the radio to complete the mission. Take control of the Sapper and throw a Grenade through the window (opposite the trapdoor) to blow up the four soldiers guarding the end of the bridge outside.

Next, move the Sniper back to the room that you found him in and look through one of the two windows ([W]) to get a view across the river. Press [A] to activate the Sniper Rifle and use [F11] to highlight enemy soldiers. Shoot soldiers [A], [B], [C], and [E] from this position. When you shoot [E], another soldier comes to investigate. Shoot him too. Move to the nearby ladder and climb it to the room above. Take advantage of this position to take out soldiers [F] and [G]. Note the positions of soldiers [D] and [H] before you cross the river.

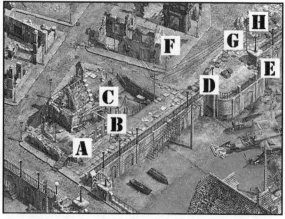

From the windows in the green wooden building, the Sniper can take out soldiers [A], [B], [C], [E], [F], and [G]. Very helpful.

Watch out for Mines hidden in the shallows of the river beyond the wire fence.

Having eliminated some of the threats on the opposite side of the river, attempt to cross it. Send your Sapper down to the water's edge at the back of the green house. Cut the wire fence using the Wirecutters, and use the Mine Detector to locate the hidden Mines in the river's shallows. Defuse these Mines and swim the Sapper across. Send the rest of your team—make sure that the Thief brings his Ladder and that one of your Commandos is still carrying the Blowtorch. Don't worry if your Sniper is running low on ammunition. You have plenty of opportunities to pick up bullets from enemy snipers stationed on this side of the river.

After you cross the river, move your squad down to the section of wall opposite the plane. Stay low at all times. Next pick off the soldiers close to the river, allowing you to get a foothold in this part of town. If you're playing the Hard or Very Hard difficulty levels, expect extra soldiers in addition to those mentioned here. Take control of the Sniper and shoot soldiers J and K. Move along the riverbank and climb up onto the jetty. Go up the steps and shoot soldier H in the bunker. Take control of the Green Beret. Use his Rifle to shoot soldier I and then D. Finally, bring up the Thief to unlock the metal crate near the bunker. Take the two Remote-Controlled Bombs and the Sniper Rifle ammo.

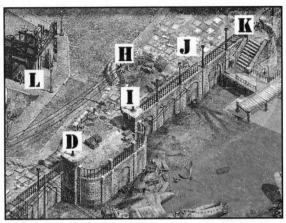

Because you need to get into the town above, kill the guards closest to the river.

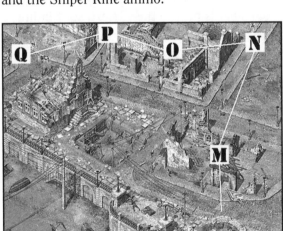

Move through the shattered buildings (M) to kill the sniper at N. Continue clearing the town via O, P, and Q.

When you control this end of town, move through the buildings as shown, starting with the shattered ruins of M. Use the Green Beret to stab any isolated soldiers. Otherwise, lead with the Sniper and use his stealthy, long-range sharp-shooting ability to pick off enemy soldiers. Clear M of German defenders—the higher the difficulty level you play, the more targets you face. Note the sniper at N. Kill him using the Sniper and search his body for extra ammunition. The key to this part of the town is to identify *where* the enemy soldiers are and *what* they can see.

Turn your attention to building **O**. Several enemy soldiers are using it for cover. Again, attack with a combination of Sniper and Rifle fire. Lead with the Sniper and attack the building from behind. Use the Thief to unlock the metal crate here and give the Grenades you find inside to the Sapper. Zoom out ((−)) to get a better view of the battlefield.

Although there are a lot of German soldiers in town, they are occupied fighting the Allied troops in the church.

The Sniper is vital as you clear this side of the town. Grab ammo from the dead enemy snipers as you go.

Another two snipers are stationed around building **P**. Shoot them and the guards next to them. Next, start killing the soldiers (**Q**) attacking the Allied soldiers. Ultimately, the only live enemies remaining are the soldiers guarding the wooden bridge in the map's corner. Before you rescue Private Smith, locate and unlock the metal crate in the hole next to the church. It contains a Bazooka, another Remote-Controlled Bomb, and some more Sniper Rifle ammunition.

Before you approach the building defended by the Allied soldiers, secure the rest of the town by killing soldiers R, S, T, and U. Stay low, so the soldier hiding on the bridge does not spot you. Use the Green Beret to stab soldier R on the metal stairway. Switch to the Sniper and have him shoot soldier S from the same stairway. Once S has been taken care of, take control of the Green Beret again and use him to stab soldiers T and U. Alternately, use the Sniper to take them out from a distance. Finally, use the Sniper to kill the soldier near the guard hut on the bridge.

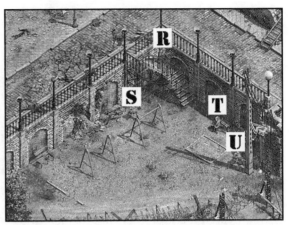

Use the Green Beret and the Sniper to take out the soldiers guarding the end of the wooden bridge.

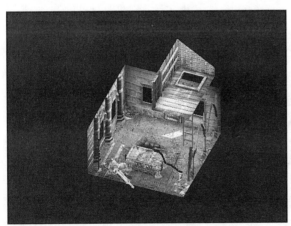

Private Smith is inside the church. Heal him with a First Aid Kit.

Give the Thief a First Aid Kit. Guide him into the church via the small hole. Use a First Aid Kit on the wounded private and then take control of him. Note that the Grenadier with him also carries a Bazooka. Give this to the Sapper later to increase his ammo. Have the Thief unlock the main door leading out of the building. A tunnel leads through the sewers and out onto the riverbank. Unfortunately, it leads to soldiers you've yet to kill on the riverbank.

As things are a little quiet, find the remaining **bonus** photo piece. By collecting it, you can play a bonus invasion mission once this level is completed. Following this walkthrough you should already have found five. The final piece can be found in the crashed bomber that lies in the river. Use the Sapper and the Blowtorch on the severed rear of the aircraft. This leads you inside—careful, two soldiers are inside. Carry a Rifle and kill them. Find the bonus photo piece in the large cabinet.

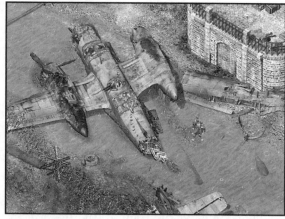

The last **bonus** photo piece is inside the crashed bomber. Use the Blowtorch to cut open the broken tail.

Cross over the wooden bridge and move toward the wrecked tank close to the riverbank. Guide Private Smith to the radio room.

To complete the mission (and, if you've collected all of the **bonus** photo pieces, to activate the bonus), guide Private Smith from the church where you found him to the radio room in the basement of the green wooden house. To get there, kill the soldiers on the opposite side of the wooden bridge. Lead with the Sniper, and use him to kill the enemy soldiers stationed around the bridge and the wrecked tank on the riverbank. When you reach the radio room, select Private Smith, press (Shift), and click the radio to finish the mission.

MISSION SECRET

Bonus photo pieces required: 6

Your objectives in this bonus section are to resist an enemy counterattack and destroy the four tanks that support it. You fail the mission if too many Allied soldiers are killed, so prepare before you click the "Launch Invasion" icon at the bottom of the screen. Using the Sapper, locate the wrecked tank next to the river. Use the Mine Detector to search the ground in front of the tank. Locate and defuse the two Anti-Tank Mines and pick them up.

Position your troops on the bridge so that they can lay down covering fire in both directions.

Move a Commando close to the Allied soldiers in the church so you can control them. Position the soldiers on the bridge. Order them to provide covering fire along its length in both directions—four facing one way, three the other. When the attack happens, the Allied soldiers can defend themselves easily.

Move your own troops between the Allied defenders. Finally, take control of the Sapper and lay Anti-Tank Mines at A, B, and C. Plant the Remote-Controlled Bomb at D.

The invasion comes from several directions at once. Kill as many soldiers as possible without losing your men or a significant number of the Allied soldiers. The first wave of soldiers appears from E and F, the second from G. The third wave of soldiers enters from the previous locations plus H and I across the river. The Anti-Tank Mines destroy three of the four tanks that accompany the invasion. Keep an eye out for the fourth one— the Sapper needs to detonate the Remote-Controlled Bomb manually.

If the enemy tanks get through, you won't survive. Plant Anti-Tank Mines and a Remote-Controlled Bomb to destroy them.

CHAPTER 14
CASTLE COLDITZ

PRIMARY OBJECTIVES

- Retrieve the Code Book from General Heinz
- Retrieve the Code Template from Field Marshall Desfell
- Retrieve the Encrypted Plan from Major General Rudolf
- Rescue the Thief without setting off the alarm
- Join the three parts of the secret plan and transmit it via the Allied radio
- Escape in the balloon

SECONDARY OBJECTIVES

- Distribute enemy uniforms to the prisoners

MISSION WALKTHROUGH

Castle Colditz is an enormous map. The infamous prison itself has over 100 rooms to explore. If that isn't difficult enough, your Commandos (the Green Beret, Spy, Driver, Sapper, and Thief) all start in separate locations. The first four are located outside the castle walls. The Thief's situation, on the other hand, is much more desperate—he's been captured and faces a firing squad. You have little, bar the Commando's standard equipment and your wits, to use in breaking into the castle. If it looks daunting, that's because it *is* daunting.

Start with the Green Beret, moving him behind the nearby haystack, and then dodging the patrolling guard to sneak to the side of the greenhouse. Use the Decoy to lure the guards away from their positions, then place the Decoy within earshot of the first guard (**A**). Activate it to draw the guard in, then deactivate it. When the guard turns to walk away, sneak up and stab him. Kill the second patrolling guard (**B**) the same way. Search the second guard for Cigarettes, which will allow you to lure one of the two Lieutenants away from their position (**C**). Simply sneak up and stab the last Lieutenant. Finally, take care of the guard (**D**) patrolling in front of the large house.

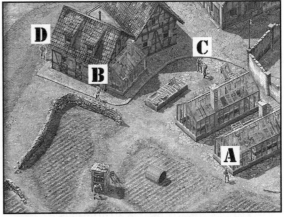

With your forces split, your first task should be to join together before you infiltrate the castle.

Move the Sniper across the bridge to join the Green Beret.

Switch to the Sniper. Knock out and tie-up the nearest guard (**E**) when his compatriots are looking the other way. Entice guard **F** from his position on the dirt track using the Sniper's Cigarettes. Next, move across the road to the small building and entice guard **G** away from the bridge. There's nothing of real interest in the building, so move on. Don't forget to search every corpse.

Take out the sniper who has a view of the bridge from the walls of the castle. There is a second sniper in the window of the castle that you can choose to take out, although he will not spot you if you're hidden. Shoot guard **H** across the river when he's at the lower end of his patrol route. Next, take out the soldiers at **I** on top of the building. Cross the bridge, taking care not to be spotted by the guard at the end of it. Double back, crawl under the bridge via **J** and head towards the Green Beret, past the body of soldier **H**. Shoot another soldier on your way to link up with the Green Beret.

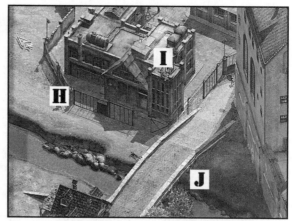

The Sniper needs to take out key soldiers before he can make his way unnoticed towards the Green Beret's location.

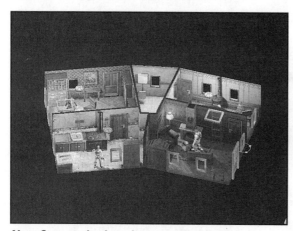

Your Commandos have been traveling light—stock up on weapons and items before you take on the castle.

Take control of the Green Beret and kill the guard standing next to the bus shelter. Follow the road around to locate the next patrolling guard. Lure him away from his normal route with Cigarettes. There are three buildings near the Green Beret's start point. Leave the two smaller buildings and investigate the larger one.

Enter the house via its side entrance, killing the Officer in the first room. Check the cupboard to find Binoculars, Poison, and a Trap. Pick up the Poison; the Spy will need it later. Next, kill the man wandering around in his underwear—the cupboard in this room contains some Cigarettes, and the bathroom has some Poison. Double-back and kill the two soldiers in the kitchen—they are unarmed and won't raise the alarm. Two Officers remain. If you enter their room via the kitchen, you can search two cupboards without being seen. Kill the Officers with the Machinegun (aim between them), then kill the two guards who climb down from the rooms above.

Switch to the Driver and lure the patrolling guard away from his route using Cigarettes. Steal the guard's machinegun and his Uniform. Don the Uniform to walk past the guard standing on the wall above. Walk behind the staff car and the small church to hide in the trees next to the ramp. Lure the guard standing opposite the ramp using Cigarettes. Knock him out, tie him up, and hide his body in the trees. Watch out for the three-man patrol walking around the town. Knock out the guard next to the ramp, tie him up, and hide his body with the other one.

The Driver can sneak past the guard on the wall by wearing a German Soldier's Uniform.

Watch out for the three-man patrol when you guide the Spy out of the large church to join the Driver.

NOTE
If you burn a critical enemy, you can't collect items off him.

NOTE
Driver cannot use Officer's Uniform—*only* Soldier's Uniform.

Take control of the Spy. Look through the main door (W) and wait until the patrol has passed. When the coast is clear, move the Spy to join the Driver in the trees. Switch to the Driver, then move him behind the small church and up behind the staff car. Kill the two Lieutenants with a Molotov Cocktail, then use the Driver to knock out and tie up the two guards standing in front of the small church. There are reinforcements inside the church, so don't venture inside.

Dress the Spy in a German Soldier's Uniform and get into the staff car. Drive it up the ramp and through the gatehouse toward the door that leads into the castle. Get out of the car and walk into the courtyard beyond. Head straight across the courtyard (ignoring the Thief, the firing squad, and the Lieutenant) to go through the small door in the wooden gates opposite. Walk across the area beyond and through the only other door. In the next room, head down the stairway.

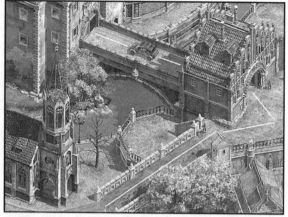

Surely only a madman would attempt to infiltrate the Colditz castle by the FRONT door!

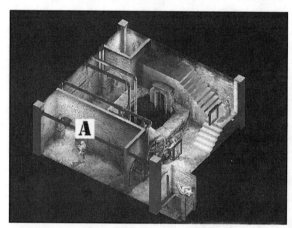

The Spy can't punch the guards he encounters. But two jabs from the Syringe has the same effect.

In the larger room beyond, locate the guard (**A**) patrolling the corridor opposite the stairway. Knock out this guard with two jabs from the Spy's Syringe. Search the unconscious guard and relieve him of his keys and Rifle. Use the key to unlock the door, which opens into the area of town where the Green Beret and the Sniper have been lurking. Move the Green Beret and the Sniper through the door and into the castle, using the Green Beret to stab the unarmed soldier. Drop prone and crawl upstairs.

In the room above, use the Spy to distract the patrolling guard, while the Green Beret creeps up and quietly knocks out and ties up the two other soldiers. Stab the soldier who has been distracted by the Spy, then search the dead bodies and the furniture for extra items. Go through the door that *doesn't* lead outside. Ignore the stairway and go through the other doorway that does lead outside. Move across to the only other door, sending the Spy in first. Draw one of the two soldiers behind the other using Cigarettes. Use the Spy's Syringe to drug and disable the guard. Kill the final guard.

After you open the locked door to admit the Green Beret, look for the three parts of the plan.

Upgrade the Spy's disguise from a Lieutenant's Uniform to an Officer's Uniform as soon as you can.

Follow the stairs up, leading with the disguised Spy. Distract the soldier in the corner so he can't see the Lieutenant at the window. Bring up the Green Beret and stab the two men. Upgrade the Spy's disguise by stealing the dead Lieutenant's Uniform, then send the Spy up the stairway. There are some more soldiers here. Use the Spy to distract the moving soldier, then position yourself so that the distracted soldier is facing away from the stairway. Again, bring up the Green Beret and kill the soldiers.

Send the Spy through the door directly opposite the end of the stairway. This is where you'll find Field Marshall Desfell. Throw a pack of Cigarettes into the corner of the room, behind the soldier near the gun cabinet. This will attract the General. If the Spy has enough Poison remaining, drug the General and tie him up. If not, bring up the Green Beret when the Spy has thrown the Cigarettes into the corner. Use the Green Beret to kill the remaining German troops. Search the coat in the corner to get the Code Template.

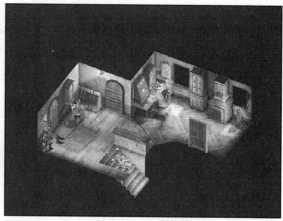

Field Marshall Desfell is the guardian of the first part of the plan—the Code Template.

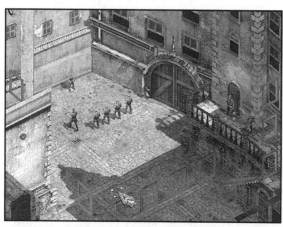

If the alarm is raised, the firing squad will instantly shoot the Thief.

Send the Spy into the stairwell and use the Distract & Disable method to kill the soldiers patrolling the area. When the area is clear, move the Spy down to the bottom of the stairwell and through the doorway. In the corridor beyond, distract the soldier and kill him using the Green Beret. The other door here leads out into the courtyard where the Thief is facing the firing squad. Go through the doorway and walk across the courtyard to leave the castle grounds. Watch the movement of the Lieutenant. Move the Green Beret outside when the Lieutenant's back is turned.

You now need to sneak the Driver inside. Wait until the Lieutenant has joined the soldiers in the square, then distract the soldier guarding the gateway to the castle. When the Lieutenant's back is turned, use the Green Beret to stalk and kill him, then to stab the guard outside the nearby building. Kill the distracted soldier and then distract and kill the guard at the top of the ramp. Having cleared this area, move the Driver from his position outside the small church to join the Green Beret and the Spy. Watch out for the patrol as you move, then position the three Commandos near the castle door.

You've broken INTO the castle, now break OUT to sneak the Driver in.

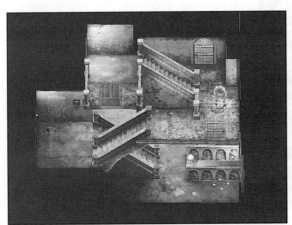

When you attack the firing squad, you MUST kill the commanding Lieutenant in your first attack. But you need the Driver.

When the Lieutenant in command of the firing squad isn't looking, move the Commandos back through the lower doorway one-by-one. Guide the group back into the large stairwell and move to the top level. Send the Spy through the doorway to the left of the stairs. Wait until the patrolling guard reaches the top of the wooden walkway and then distract him. Send in the Green Beret to kill the distracted guard and the second guard working on the cannons below. Look through the door into the mess hall beyond.

The mess hall is filled with soldiers. Even the Spy will be spotted if he's not careful. Wait until the white-shirted man leaves to join his comrades, then crawl the Green Beret across the room, keeping as close to the far side as you can. You should be able to make it all the way across and into the corridor beyond. Repeat this process for the other members of your team. Quicksave the game before you make each attempt— just in case. Should the alarm go off, the firing squad will open fire on the Thief in the courtyard below and you'll have to restart the mission.

Take care when you cross the mess hall. There are Officers here who will see through even the Spy's disguise.

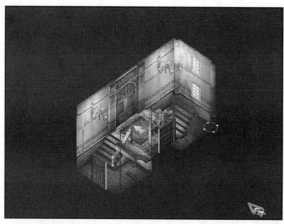

If you get lost in the castle, bring up the Notebook and click on the objective you wish to complete. An 'Objective' icon will appear onscreen. Clicking it brings up a yellow arrow showing you which way to go.

In the room beyond the mess hall, take the stairway down. If you get lost at any point, call up the Notebook and highlight the objective featuring General Heinz. Click on the Objective icon when it appears onscreen and the game will display a bright yellow arrow that points toward the next objective. In the stairwell below, send the Spy through the large double doors and into the room beyond.

The Code Book is located in another coat in the corner of the room. The trick is getting there without being spotted—there are two Officers at the end of the room, either of which can see through your disguise. Start by distracting the Lieutenant on the right of the room. Bring in the Green Beret and knock out the white-shirted soldier. Your chance to knock out the second Lieutenant will come when he pauses to look out of the window. Finally, kill the distracted Lieutenant. Lure the Officer who is *not* looking at the coat stand (General Heinz himself) into the corner with Cigarettes and knock him out as well. Creep up behind the remaining Officer and stab him. Search the coat to find the Code Book. Grab an Officer's Uniform for the Spy.

General Heinz looks after the second part of the plan—the Code Book.

You need to kill the soldier on the balcony before you can attack the firing squad.

Look through the wooden door to the right of the room you've just left. This should give you a view of the inner courtyard where the Thief is facing the firing squad. Send the Spy through the door and distract the soldier outside. When the Lieutenant in charge of the firing squad isn't looking (i.e. he stands at the end of the line), send in the Green Beret to stab the distracted soldier. Remove the body before the Lieutenant looks back.

You can't distract the guards or the Lieutenant to free the Thief—as soon as you mess with the firing squad, they open fire. Swap back to the Driver and arm him with a Molotov Cocktail and a Rifle with at least three bullets. When the Lieutenant walks back to join the line of soldiers, throw a Molotov at the Soldier standing next to him. Three soldiers should be caught in the fiery blast. Take the remaining two out with the Rifle. Free the Thief by talking to him—don't worry about the alarm, it will fall silent eventually. Start stripping the Soldiers of their clothes. You have more objectives: distribute Uniforms to the prisoners so they can escape, combine the three parts of the plans, and use the Allied radio.

Free the Thief by aiming a Molotov Cocktail at the end of the firing squad. Shoot any guards that survive the initial blast.

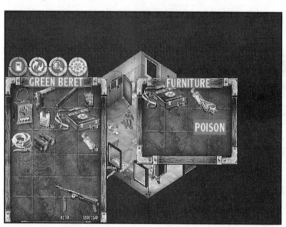

Pick up bottles of Poison wherever you find them. The Spy needs as much ammunition as he can find.

You have one last piece of the plan to find. Send the Spy through the small door on the same side of the wall as the door you entered the courtyard by. Walk through the corridor and into the large stairwell from earlier. Climb the stairs to the middle level and head back into the room where you picked up the Code Template and killed Field Marshall Desfell. This time, however, move through the door opposite the coat stand. Walk through the infirmary beyond and search it to find more Poison—you need at least six doses. Go through the only other door and you'll find yourself on a walkway, high above the inner courtyard.

There are two Officers and a soldier in the room beyond. Open the door and move away from the doorway. Distract the pacing Officer when the white-shirted soldier is on the other side of the room. Jab him twice with the Syringe and tie him up. Next, take care of the white-shirted Soldier in the same way. Monitor the vision of the last remaining Officer (Major General Rudolf), and creep around behind him when he stops to read. Jab and tie him up. Search the coat stand in the corner to get the Encrypted Map. You now have all three parts of the plan.

The prisoners are held in the opposite side of the castle from the one you have been walking around in. Move the Commandos to join the Spy, killing any soldiers along the way and stealing their Uniforms. Don't use any guns—this will only bring reinforcements running. Move quietly, past the room where you found the Encrypted Map. Kill the guard at the bottom of the stairway outside Major General Rudolf's office. Head down the stairway and into the room beyond. Distract and disable the guards, then leave via the only door. Always lead with the Spy since he can scout ahead thanks to his disguise.

The Colditz castle is split into two different parts—one half is home to the German garrison, the other is the prison itself.

This brings you to an outside area. Distract and kill the guard, robbing him of his Uniform. There's a doorway and an archway here. Try the doorway first. Lead with the Spy and distract and disable the guards inside. Next, head up the stairs and take out the Soldier and the Officer. Head back down the stairs and out to join the others. Now take the archway that leads into another inner courtyard. Bring your team into the courtyard and send the Spy into building Ⓐ.

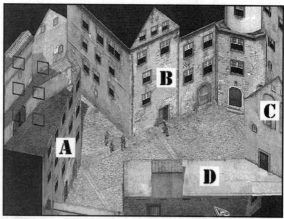

You need to free 50 Allied prisoners to complete the mission objective.

Enter building Ⓐ first. This building has three rows of four windows above its doorway.

Your Commandos can hold up to 30 Uniforms, 10 of each type—Soldier, Lieutenant and Officer. To give one to any Allied prisoners you find, press Ⓦ to activate the Examine command, and then click on the prisoner to open his inventory. Simply drag and drop the Uniform. Hold (Shift) if you want to drag a single Uniform from a pile of Uniforms that you have in your inventory. When the prisoner is unguarded, he will make his own escape. Work through the buildings here using a combination of the Spy and the Green Beret. They make a great team.

In building **A**, you'll find a total of 14 prisoners. There are four on the ground floor, one in the corridor, and three in the chapel. On the first floor, above the chapel, you'll find another four. There are five more POWs on the floor above. Again, distract the guards using the Spy and kill them using the Green Beret. There's one more in the roof. Reach him by climbing the ladder.

Move next door to building **B**. This building has four doors and 18 prisoners held inside. Behind the first door, you'll find four POWs cleaning the showers on the ground floor. Kill the soldier that guards them. Head into the second door and kill the soldier patrolling the ground floor level. There are six prisoners on the first floor. Take your time and clear it of enemy guards, freeing the POWs as you go. Head up the stairway to the second floor. There are two more prisoners here—free them without alerting the guards. Finally, climb the ladder to free the two POWs in the attic. Leave this part of the building. There are no POWs behind door three (although this leads to the bell tower and the radio.

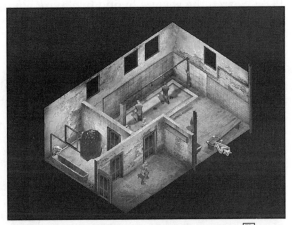

There are more POWs to be freed in building **B** next door, so make sure you strip the soldiers that you kill of their Uniforms.

The fourth door (a set of double doors, really) leads into a shattered theatre. There's a single POW on the stage. Enter building **C** via the stage door near the POW you have just freed. There are three prisoners in this area—two in the gym, another in a small room on the other side of the room layout. Head up the stairway; there are three POWs on this first floor. Go up another level to find two more. Search the shelves to find three **bonus** picture pieces. Go up the stairs again onto the next floor. There are two more POWs here and four more **bonus** photo pieces.

Head through the door into a series of green-walled rooms to find six POWs. Free them and search the furniture to find two **bonus** photo pieces. Finally, climb the ladder to reach the attic above. Give Uniforms to the two POWs that you find here. Return to the courtyard and enter building **D**—it has a flat roof. You'll find two prisoners on this ground floor plus one **bonus** photo piece. Head down to the basement to free another POW. Search the shelves to find two more **bonus** pieces. Check your Notebook to see whether enough prisoners have been freed.

Now all you need to do is make your way back to the courtyard and take the door that leads to the bell tower and the radio. Kill the guards inside. Make sure that the Green Beret has all three parts of the plan and that they have been combined into one item. Use the radio to inform the Allies of the German's plan to blow up Paris. Leave the radio room and return to the inner courtyard, leaving the courtyard via the archway. The Allies have provided you with a balloon so you can make your escape.

Use the radio (located in the bell tower), then guide your troops out of the castle to the balloon.

To play the bonus mission, collect the remaining **bonus** pieces from the following locations. There are seven pieces in the shop (**1**), and three more in the small building behind it (**2**). You'll find another two in building **3** that has a small greenhouse, and three in building **4**. There are also two **bonus** photo pieces to be found in the factory near the Green Beret's start point—the one that has three chimneys.

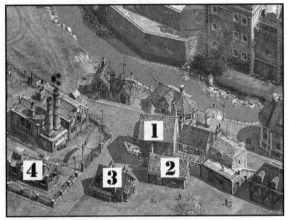

If you want to play the bonus mission after this Colditz mission, you need to find the remaining pieces of the **bonus** photograph.

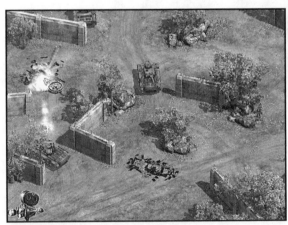

The Sapper provides the gunnery support for the Driver.

MISSION SECRET

Bonus photo pieces required: 31

This mission involves tank-to-tank combat—it's good practice for the Paris mission that follows. Move the Driver and Sapper into the tank that has been provided for you. The tank can be driven around the battlefield using the four cursor keys. Pressing Ctrl activates the gunnery sight and shells can be fired with a single left-click of the mouse button. Destroy all of the armored units to complete the bonus mission.

CHAPTER 15

IS PARIS BURNING?

PRIMARY OBJECTIVES	SECONDARY OBJECTIVES
• Disconnect the detonator in General's office	• Obtain Mines and Grenades
• Contact Natasha	• Steal a tank
• Use the radio at the top of the tower	• Obtain the key for the lower tower from the SS General

MISSION WALKTHROUGH

In this final mission, you control all of the main characters—Green Beret, Sniper, Diver, Sapper, Driver, Spy, Thief, Natasha, and even Whiskey the dog. Moving them around en masse is hardly a sound tactic. In this mission, they operate in ones and twos. For example, the Sapper and the Driver, or Spy and Green Beret, make good teams. Despite its huge size, this mission isn't quite as hard as you might think.

Take control of the Green Beret. Move him onto the platform and behind the small kiosk. Kill the soldier sitting on the stool when the patrolling guard walks away. Hide the body inside the kiosk. Next, kill the patrolling guard, followed by the soldier on the bench. Finally, attack the two soldiers working on the subway tracks. Before you leave this area, search the wastebasket near the exit to find the first piece of the bonus photograph.

Start this mission with the Green Beret. Use him to kill all of the soldiers in the subway.

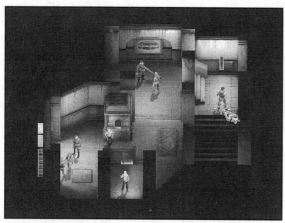

Use the Green Beret and the Spy (dressed in a Lieutenant's Uniform) to kill the soldiers in this area.

Dress the Spy in the Lieutenant's Uniform and send him upstairs. Distract the nearest guard so he's not looking directly at the doorway, then bring up the Green Beret and kill the guard when the patrolling Lieutenant walks out of range. Place the body at the end of the corridor and wait for the patrolling Lieutenant to spot it. Stab him when he's close enough. Use the Spy to distract the soldier facing the man on the stool, then use the Green Beret to stab both white-shirted soldiers. Finally, arm the Green Beret with the Machinegun and aim at the last two guards. The wide-angle fire should nail them both.

Send the Spy out through the only exit. Zoom out to see what you have to deal with. You should see patrolling guards on either side of the subway entrance, plus a Lieutenant and a soldier nearby. An armored car regularly swings by too, just to make things complicated. Your first task is to contact Natasha.

Zoom out to discover the positions of the enemy soldiers in this part of the map.

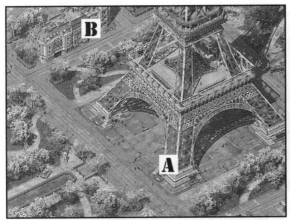

Attack the sniper at **A** to get more Sniper Rifle ammunition before you head toward the building and a rendezvous with Natasha.

Leave your Commando squad in the subway and guide the Spy toward the building next to the Eiffel Tower. Keep to the roads and stay away from enemy soldiers in case higher-ranking officers see through your disguise. En route, use the Syringe on the sniper at the base of the tower (**A**). Steal his Sniper Rifle to give to the Sniper later. When you reach the large building, enter via door **B**.

Walk into the room and use the elevator. Natasha is on the building's top floor, so ride all the way up and press $\boxed{X}$ to leave the elevator car. Talk to Natasha and note the extra mission objectives—get the key to the Eiffel Tower from the SS Officer and use the radio at the top of the tower. Controlling the Spy *and* Natasha, walk back to the elevator and out of the building.

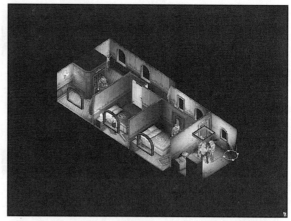

Once freed, Natasha tells you the rest of the mission objectives—deactivate the detonator and use the radio at the top of the tower.

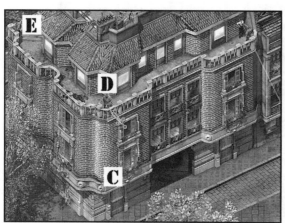

Kill the snipers on the roof now so they can't attack you later when you steal the nearby tank.

Before you make the long journey back to the subway entrance, walk in via door $\boxed{C}$, collecting a Poison bottle from the first floor. Ignore the second floor for now, but search the furniture on the third floor for another Poison bottle. Take the two **bonus** pieces on this floor. Climb the stairs to the top floor, drop the Spy prone, and use the Syringe to dispatch snipers $\boxed{D}$ and $\boxed{E}$. Attack $\boxed{E}$ when the patrolmen below have their backs to you. Search the dead sharp-shooters to get Sniper Rifle ammunition.

Give the extra Sniper Rifle ammo to the Sniper. Use Natasha and the Spy to distract the two guards (**F**) nearest the subway entrance. Bring up the Sniper (crawling so he's not spotted), then wait until the armored car has driven past on its long loop and shoot the guard (**G**) patrolling on the opposite side of the two guards. An Officer (**H**) may come to investigate—hold your position and shoot him, too. Move toward the distracted guards (**F**) and shoot the soldier (**I**) patrolling the path nearby, plus the Lieutenant if he sees you do it. Finally, deal with the distracted guards (**F**). Watch out for the armored car at all times. If it spots you, it will open fire.

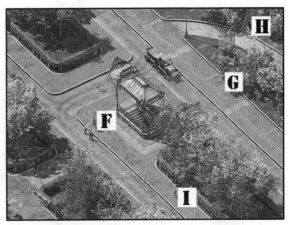

Use the Sniper to kill the soldiers immediately surrounding the subway entrance.

To move around safely, use the Spy to steal the truck at position **J**.

When this area is clear, grab the Officer's Uniform from **H** and dress the Spy in it. Guide the Spy toward the truck (**J**) parked next to the metal crates. Jump in and drive it back to the subway entrance. Load the Thief, Natasha, Sapper, and Driver into the back of the truck, then drive back to the place where you found the truck. Make sure that the Spy remains in the truck (as its driver) so he can protect the passengers. If he gets out, the Commandos inside will be spotted instantly.

Park the truck close to the crates, but don't touch the barrels or they'll explode, taking the truck out too. Monitor the vision of the three soldiers near the truck. Use Natasha to distract the soldier who looks at the back of the truck. A guard regularly patrols the path beyond the crates (**K**). Place a View Marker on the metal crates and move the Thief out of the truck when guard **K** isn't watching. Use the Thief to unlock the crates, watching out for that patrolling guard. Take the Timed Bombs, Remote-Controlled Bombs, Grenades, and the Anti-Tank Mines that you find there.

When you back up the truck, DON'T hit any of the barrels. They'll explode and take your truck (and Commandos) out with them.

You must disable the tank (**M**) and the armored car before you can safely drive around in the spare tank (**L**).

When you have plundered the crates, jump back into the truck and drive back to the subway entrance. Use the Sapper to plant an Anti-Tank Mine in the road and wait for the armored car to drive over it. Replace the Thief with the Sniper. Next, steal the unmanned tank (**L**) near the large building. Make sure you have the Sapper and the Driver in the back of the truck.

Drive the truck toward the unmanned tank (), then back it up into the open area as shown. When the active tank (M) has driven by, take control of the Sapper and plant a second Anti-Tank Mine on the pathway between the trees—take care not to be spotted by the German guard on the grass. The tank will roll over it on its next pass and be destroyed.

Plant an Anti-Tank Mine on the path just between the trees in the nearby park. This will destroy the tank.

Use the Sniper to kill most of the soldiers surrounding the unmanned tank (L).

When tank M has been destroyed, move the Sniper out of the truck and shoot the soldiers around tank L. Start with the soldier on the street corner as shown. Shoot the soldiers who run to investigate his death. Finally shoot the Lieutenant and any soldiers around tank L itself. Move the Driver and the Sapper into the tank. Don't worry if the alarm is raised—the tank is bulletproof and you have taken care of the armored car and tank that could have destroyed it. Press Ctrl to activate the tank's big gun.

Move around the map as you kill soldiers. Highlight enemies with [F11]. Either blast the enemy with the tank's cannon or simply run over any soldiers that you come across. Overkill? Of course it is. You can even kill any remaining snipers on the roof of the large building. Once you've taken out most of the external threats, use the Green Beret, Diver, and Thief to collect Machineguns from dead soldiers.

Move the Driver into the tank to control it and move the Sapper in to act as the gunner.

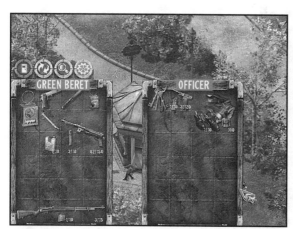

The only way to get into the Eiffel Tower and complete the mission is to steal the SS Officer's keys.

Pick up the keys to the tower from the dead Officer. Press [F10] to locate him—dead bodies with useful items on them are highlighted in green. When you have the key and your Commandos are well armed with Machineguns, turn your attention to the large building. Not only is the explosive detonator located in here, but it's also where you'll find most of the bonus photo pieces.

NOTE

Bonus pieces are always found in furniture, never on enemy soldiers or in wooden boxes or crates.

Go through door C again. Lead with the Spy and follow up with the Diver, Sapper, Green Beret, and Thief. There's nothing of interest on the first floor, so move up to the floor above. Distract the guard patrolling near the stairway. Kill him and use the Sapper to throw a Grenade through the side door, killing the Generals inside. Use a Commando with a Machinegun to kill the remaining soldiers. Then use the Sapper to disable the detonator, then search the dead bodies and furniture for extra items.

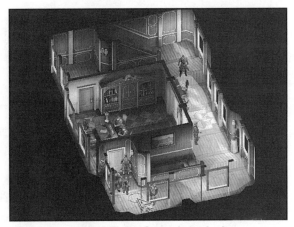

Use a Grenade to kill the Generals in the large building. Use the Sapper to disarm the explosive detonator here.

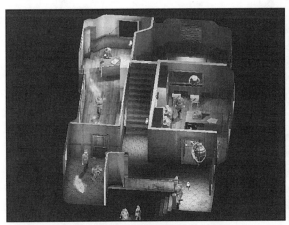

Work your way through the building, killing its occupants and searching for pieces of the **bonus** photo.

Head up to the third floor, Spy first. Use the Spy to distract the nearest soldier and then kill him. Position a Machinegunner in front of the two rooms here and use the Sapper to throw a Grenade into the room near the stairway. Once you've killed everyone, search the dead bodies and the furniture to find two pieces of the **bonus** photo (if you haven't already taken them). Send the Spy up to the top floor, bringing up the rest of your squad. Kill everyone and pick up the **bonus** photo piece. Kill any snipers that remain on the roof.

Return to the first floor and enter the other half of the building via door **B**. Kill the soldiers inside and search the furniture to find another piece of the **bonus** photo. You find two **bonus** pieces on the second floor, plus another two on the third floor. The elevator doesn't work. Send the Thief to the roof of the building, fully armed with Rifle and Machinegun.

If you want to play the bonus mission at the end of this one, search the large building thoroughly.

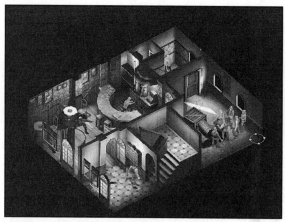

Eight more pieces of the **bonus** photo are in the building's central section.

Finally, enter the middle section of the large building via the glass door on the opposite side. Find eight pieces of the **bonus** photo here: one piece on the first floor, two on the second floor, four on the third floor, and one more on the fourth floor. All but one of the **bonus** pieces (which is located in the subway) are in this large building.

To complete the mission, give the SS Officer's keys to the Spy and send him across to one of the entrances marked "E" at the base of the Eiffel Tower. Open the door with the keys and use the elevator to go up as far as it takes you. Leave that car and enter the central part of the tower to take another elevator car up. Keep climbing (using ladders when the elevator has risen as high as it can go), and use the radio at the very top of the tower itself.

Use the Spy to infiltrate the Eiffel Tower and activate the radio at the top of it.

MISSION SECRET

Bonus photo pieces required: 17

The Commandos need to cross the enemy lines and escape in the German staff car. Along the way, you need to neutralize the enemy snipers, obtain some Wirecutters to open the fence, and enter the bunker to stop the alarm being raised. For this mini-mission, you command the Green Beret, Sniper, Driver, and Thief.

Move the Sniper up to this side of the other bombed-out building (**A**). Creep forward and shoot the enemy sniper (**B**) before he can shoot you. Shoot the soldier (**C**) next to the metal crate. Send the Thief through the fence toward the metal crate. Unlock and open it to get the Wirecutters, a Shovel, and some Molotov Cocktails. Crawl the Sniper forward and take out the guard (**D**) next to the supplies behind the trench.

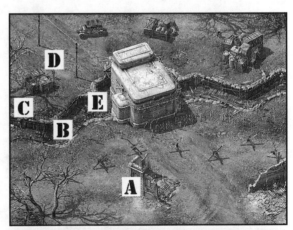

To attack these German lines, approach from the left side, heading toward the metal crate.

Shoot the Officer when he investigates and then the Lieutenant ([E]). Cut open the wire fencing and move the squad into the trench.

Knock out and tie up the guard sitting outside the bunker's main door. Take control of the Thief and climb up to the left window above the door. Look through it ([W]) before you enter. Knock out the Officer and take his keys. Move into the next room quickly. Knock out the soldier and then climb down the ladder to the room below. The two soldiers in this room are too busy to notice you. Open the door, stun the soldier reading the paper, and unlock the door. Send in the Green Beret or the Driver to knock out and tie up the guards on the ground floor. Throw a Molotov at the men in the side room. Finally, kill the men on the top floor and get the Sniper Rifle.

Bring up the Sniper. Stock up on ammunition and use the Sniper to kill the remaining soldiers. When everyone is dead, move your team into the staff car and drive it offscreen.